Farmhouse Weekends

Farmhouse Weekends

Menus for Relaxing Country Meals All Year Long

MELISSA BAHEN
CREATOR OF **Lulu the Baker**

GIBBS SMITH
TO ENRICH AND INSPIRE HUMANKIND

First Edition
27 26 25 24   10 9 8 7

Published by
Gibbs Smith
P.O. Box 667
Layton, Utah 84041

1.800.835.4993 orders
www.gibbs-smith.com

Illustrations by Celeste Rockwood-Jones
Designed by Michelle Farinella
Printed and bound in China
Gibbs Smith books are printed on either recycled, 100% post-consumer waste, FSC-certified papers or on paper produced from sustainable PEFC-certified forest/controlled wood source. Learn more at www.pefc.org.

Library of Congress Cataloging-in-Publication Data

Names: Bahen, Melissa, author.
Title: Farmhouse weekends : menus for relaxing country meals all year long / Melissa Bahen.
Description: First edition. | Layton : Gibbs Smith, [2021]
Identifiers: LCCN 2020033174 | ISBN 9781423656722 (hardcover) | ISBN 9781423656739 (epub)
Subjects: LCSH: Cooking, American. | LCGFT: Cookbooks.
Classification: LCC TX715 .B14825 2021 | DDC 641.5973—dc23
LC record available at https://lccn.loc.gov/2020033174

For the loves of my life:

Speedy, Addie, Ellie, James, and Georgie.

I love you forever and ever.

autumn

winter

Introduction

SOME PEOPLE DAYDREAM about relaxing, beautiful country living because they are overworked, overstretched adults. Not me. My fascination with farm life started when I was a kid. As a child, I loved reading books about living on a farm. I was enchanted by the serene, bucolic settings, the talk of planting and harvesting crops, and most importantly, the descriptions of mouthwatering, made-from-scratch farm feasts: flap jacks, hand-cranked ice cream, pies galore, biscuits and gravy, steamed peas with butter, and more. It all sounded magical—and delicious.

For basically my whole adult life, I've been trying to create that farmhouse life-style for myself, in whatever small ways I could manage at the time. When my husband and I were newlyweds living in a condo in the suburbs of Las Vegas, we tried our best to grow cherry tomatoes on our tiny patio, and canned dozens of jars of homemade jam using the apricots from my parents' backyard. When we graduated to our first stand-alone house after we started having kids, it was in a suburban neighborhood in western Oregon. We filled our postage stamp–size backyard with raised vegetable beds and fruit trees, grew corn along the fence in our side yard, and kept chickens in a little A-frame coop we bought on Craigslist. (I didn't have any friends at the time with backyard chickens—how times have changed!)

WE FINALLY MOVED INTO OUR DREAM FARMHOUSE in the country in the late fall of 2014. A white farmhouse with a wrap-around porch and modern touches, our house is surrounded by a big garden, an orchard full of fruit trees, a much bigger chicken coop, and acres for the kids to run and play on—exactly what I'd always dreamed of having. But do you want to know something? When you get down to details, our life looks largely the same as before: we can dozens of jars of homemade salsa at the end of every summer; we have fresh eggs to scramble up or mix into buttermilk pancakes for breakfast; we pick cherries in late spring and apples in the fall. And those are things you can do whether you live on a farm in the country or in a tiny apartment in a bustling metropolis.

Even though we live in the country, we aren't farmers by trade. My husband and I both have jobs that have nothing to do with farming, raising chickens, or cultivating berry bushes. During the week, we have work and community events and our kids have school and activities. My family packs its weekdays full of activities just like other families do. And on those busy days, we are grateful for meals ready in minutes. But weekends at the farmhouse are a different story entirely.

Weekends are when we get to work the soil and plant our garden, or wander the aisles of our local farmers market looking for the most beautiful fresh produce.

Weekends are when we stir bowls of ripe berries, mashed with sugar and pectin, and pour the mixture into dozens of containers, stashing a year's worth of sweet-as-candy jam in the freezer.

Weekends are when we finally have time to slow down, take a deep breath, and work on the big project we've been putting off all week, whether that's building raised garden beds, canning homemade salsa, or kneading a batch of dough for caramel sticky buns and patiently waiting for it to rise.

Weekends are about relaxing, taking time to slow down and enjoy good people, delicious food, and experiences worth savoring.

Farmhouse Weekends is a cookbook for everyone out there who daydreams of country life—to help you create and enjoy one wherever you make your home. It's for people who spend their week being busy, running errands, and working 9 to 5, but long to spend their weekends mucking about in a big vegetable patch, collecting fresh eggs from a flock of backyard chickens, or canning a few dozen jars of homemade salsa. It will inspire you to create meals and experiences to enjoy in the easy companionship of family and friends—everything you need for the perfect farmhouse weekend. Let's get started!

spring

SPRING AT THE FARMHOUSE is a time of awakening and renewal. We watch flowers slowly poke their heads out of the ground and bring some much-needed color to the landscape: first daffodils and grape hyacinths then tulips. We visit the new baby lambs on the farm and watch them run through verdant fields of new grass. We start seeds for our garden: peas, radishes, and carrots outside for late spring eating; green beans, tomatoes, and peppers in pots inside until the weather turns warm enough for them to be transplanted to the garden. The longer days mean the chickens start laying eggs again, if they stopped during the winter months, and new chicks can be heard sweetly cheeping at the local farm store. We splash in puddles, get our bikes out of storage, and collect the year's first bouquets of wildflowers. We eat tender asparagus spears as soon as they poke through the dirt, and watch the bees buzz from blossom to blossom in the orchard.

Farmhouse Weekends in the Spring

pick tulips • visit new farm babies • go strawberry picking • plant seeds
• splash in puddles • fly a kite • spin yarn from new wool • go bird watching
• make homemade farmer's cheese with fresh milk • chase butterflies
• collect and press wildflowers • ride a bike down a country lane
• shell a bushel of fresh garden peas • attend a local flower festival

Apricot, Almond & Coconut Scones

I love a good scone on a slow weekend morning. Scones combine so many of my favorite features of other baked breakfast treats, but do it in a style all their own. They are tender and buttery like a biscuit, but more crumbly than flaky. And they're much sweeter than biscuits, but not at all cakey like a muffin or slice of quick bread would be. They have craggy tops that are perfect for catching glazes and garnishes, and they taste wonderful slathered with jam. These scones bring together some of my favorite flavors—tangy apricot and smooth, tropical coconut—into an irresistible spring breakfast pastry that will have you sneaking bites all morning long. **Makes 8 scones**

For the scones

2 cups all-purpose flour

1/3 cup granulated sugar

2 teaspoons baking powder

1/4 teaspoon salt

5 ounces cold cream cheese, cut into chunks

6 tablespoons cold butter, cut into chunks

1/2 cup finely chopped dried apricots

1/2 cup sweetened coconut flakes

1/4 cup sliced almonds, lightly crushed (just with your fingers)

3 tablespoons whole milk plus 1 tablespoon for brushing on scones

1 egg

1 teaspoon vanilla extract

1/4 teaspoon almond extract

1 tablespoon coarse sugar

For the cream cheese glaze

1 ounce cream cheese, softened

1 tablespoon butter, softened

1/4 cup powdered sugar

1/4 teaspoon almond extract or vanilla extract

1 teaspoon whole milk

Toasted sliced almonds and toasted coconut for garnishing

continued

1. Preheat oven to 400°F and line a baking sheet with parchment paper.

2. In the bowl of a food processor, combine flour, granulated sugar, baking powder, and salt. Pulse 3–4 times to combine. Add the cream cheese and butter chunks, and pulse about 20 times until the butter is in small pieces no bigger than peas. Pour the mixture into a large bowl. Add the apricots, coconut, and almonds, and toss gently to combine.

3. In a small bowl or glass measuring cup, whisk 3 tablespoons milk, egg, vanilla, and almond extract until combined. Add the wet ingredients to the dry ingredients, and gently mix with a spatula until a dough forms.

4. Place the dough on a lightly floured surface, and form it into a circle about ³/4 inch thick. Cut the dough circle into 8 equal wedges, and place the wedges on the baking sheet with a couple of inches between each wedge. Refrigerate the scones for 15 minutes.

5. After the scones have chilled, brush the tops with the remaining milk then sprinkle with coarse sugar.

6. Bake for 18–20 minutes until the scones are golden brown. Remove from the oven and allow to cool while making the glaze.

7. To make the glaze, combine cream cheese and butter in a small bowl. Add powdered sugar and almond extract or vanilla, and beat until smooth. This is such a tiny amount of glaze that you don't need to use a mixer. When the glaze is smooth, add the milk, a little at a time, until the glaze is a drizzleable consistency. Use a spoon to drizzle the glaze over the scones. You can alternately put the glaze in a small, disposable plastic bag, squeeze it all into one corner, cut the very tip of the corner off, and pipe stripes of glaze onto the scones. Sprinkle toasted sliced almonds and toasted coconut on top. Serve warm or at room temperature.

Notes

1. Scones are best eaten fresh! Like biscuits, the texture is at its peak within a few hours of being made.

2. For an easy breakfast, make the scones the night before and bake them in the morning. After placing the wedges on the baking sheet, cover them with plastic wrap and refrigerate overnight. In the morning, preheat oven and go straight to step 5.

3. You can mix the dry ingredients by hand, just cut the cold cream cheese and butter in with a pastry blender.

4. Toast the sliced almonds and coconut flakes in the preheated oven while the scones chill in the fridge. Sprinkle a few tablespoons of each in a small baking dish (a pie plate works perfectly), and pop it in the oven until the coconut is golden. Watch carefully so you don't burn your garnish!

Lemon-Honey Tea Cakes
with Buttermilk Glaze

These scrumptious little cakes are like muffins' fancier cousins. They are flavored with fresh lemon and honey, their tops dunked in a tangy lemon and buttermilk glaze. My kids devour them when I make a batch. They are perfect for breakfast or dessert, or really anytime in between, and look extra sweet with a tiny flower blossom on top. **Makes 12 tea cakes**

For the cakes

1 lemon, zested

3/4 cup granulated sugar

7 tablespoons butter

7 tablespoons honey (1/4 cup plus 3 tablespoons)

1 egg

1/2 cup buttermilk

1/8 teaspoon lemon extract

2 cups all-purpose flour

1/2 teaspoon salt

1/2 teaspoon baking soda

For the glaze

1 1/2 cups powdered sugar

3 tablespoons buttermilk

A pinch of salt

1/4 teaspoon lemon extract

Up to 1 tablespoon fresh lemon juice

continued

1. Preheat oven to 300°F. Spray a 12-cup muffin tin with nonstick baking spray with flour. You can also butter and flour each well in the tin.

2. Rub the lemon zest and sugar together in a small saucepan until the mixture is fragrant and looks like wet sand. Add the butter and honey, and stir over low heat until the butter is melted, the sugar is dissolved, and the mixture is smooth except for the lemon zest. Remove from heat and set aside.

3. In a large bowl, whisk egg, buttermilk, and lemon extract.

4. In a medium bowl, combine flour, salt, and baking soda. Add half of the flour mixture to the buttermilk mixture, and whisk until just combined. Do the same with half of the butter mixture. Repeat until all the ingredients are added, whisking just until the batter is smooth.

5. Divide the batter evenly among the 12 muffin cups, and bake 22–25 minutes, until a toothpick inserted in the center of a cake comes out clean. Allow to cool in the tin for 5–10 minutes then take them out and let cool completely on a wire rack. If they don't easily pop out of the muffin tin, run a small paring knife around the edge of each cake to loosen.

6. While the tea cakes cool, make the glaze. Combine the powdered sugar, buttermilk, salt, and lemon extract in a medium bowl and whisk until completely smooth. Whisk lemon juice in, a little at a time, until the glaze is just barely thin enough for dipping. When the tea cakes are cool, dip the top of each in the glaze. Let the excess glaze drip back into the bowl then turn the cakes right side up and place back on the cooling rack. Allow the glaze to set before serving.

Note

If you spray the measuring cup and spoon with nonstick baking spray before you measure the honey, it will slide right out.

Orange Knots

The first time I ever made these was for Easter when my oldest kids were just tiny. And oh my, were they delicious! Knots of rich dough dipped in melted butter and coated in orange-scented sugar then baked until golden and drizzled with a sweet citrus glaze. There were only four of us at the time, but we ate the entire batch without much difficulty. These sweet orange breakfast pastries are so good on springtime mornings, and make Easter brunch extra special. **Makes 18 knots**

For the dough

1/4 cup warm water

1 tablespoon active dry yeast

1 cup warm milk (microwaved for about 1 minute)

1/3 cup granulated sugar

1/3 cup butter, melted (microwaved for about 1 minute)

1 teaspoon salt

1 egg

4 cups all-purpose flour

For the orange sugar

2 oranges, zested

1 cup granulated sugar

1/4 cup butter, melted and cooled

For the orange glaze

1 cup powdered sugar

3 tablespoons orange juice

1 tablespoon butter, melted

1/2 teaspoon vanilla extract

A pinch of salt

continued

1. To make the dough, combine the warm water and yeast in a small bowl or glass measuring cup. Set aside in a warm spot for 10 minutes until the yeast is activated and the mixture begins to grow in volume. Meanwhile, combine the warm milk, sugar, butter, salt, and egg in a large bowl or in the bowl of a stand mixer. Add the proofed yeast mixture and mix to combine. Add the flour. If you are using a stand mixer, switch to the dough hook attachment at this point. If you are making the bread dough in a large bowl, stir it with a wooden spoon until it gets too difficult then use your hands. Either way, knead the dough for 5 minutes until smooth and elastic. At this point, the dough might still be slightly sticky, and that's okay. Place the dough in a bowl that's been sprayed with non-stick baking spray or lightly coated with oil, cover it with a damp towel, and set in a warm place to rise until double in volume, about 1 hour.

2. While the dough is rising, prepare the orange sugar. Gently stir the orange zest and sugar together in a medium bowl and set aside.

3. When the dough has doubled in volume, remove the towel, punch down the dough, and knead it lightly on a well-floured surface for about 1 minutes. Divide the dough into 18 equal pieces. Roll each piece into a 9-inch-long rope, and tie each rope into a loose knot. Place the knots on a parchment-lined baking sheet. I do 3 rows of 6.

4. Roll a knot in melted butter then in orange sugar. Place it back on the baking sheet and repeat with the remaining knots. Cover and let rise in a warm place for 30 minutes. While the orange knots are rising, preheat the oven to 350°F.

5. Uncover the orange knots and bake for 15–18 minutes until puffed and lightly golden. While the orange knots cool, make the glaze.

6. Whisk all of the glaze ingredients in a medium bowl. Spoon glaze evenly over the orange knots when they are cool enough to touch, but still warm. Serve warm or at room temperature.

Spinach, Avocado & Snap Pea Salad with Raspberry-Shallot Vinaigrette

This salad is a feast for the belly and for the eyes. It's full of all the best offerings of a spring garden: tender spinach, sweet snap peas, juicy strawberries, piquant scallions, and peppery radishes. It's a mix of subtle shades of green accentuated with pops of ruby red and vibrant pink. **Serves 8**

For the vinaigrette

- $1/2$ cup granulated sugar
- $1/2$ cup olive oil
- $1/4$ cup raspberry vinegar
- 2 teaspoons Dijon mustard
- 1 teaspoon Worcestershire sauce
- 1 teaspoon finely chopped shallot
- 1 teaspoon paprika
- A pinch of kosher salt

For the candied almonds

- 1 cup slivered almonds
- 2 tablespoons granulated sugar
- A pinch of salt

For the salad

- 1 (5-ounce) package baby spinach
- 2 small avocados, diced
- 1 bunch scallions, thinly sliced on the diagonal, white and light green parts only
- 1 bunch radishes, thinly sliced
- $1/2$ pound strawberries, sliced (about $1 1/2$ cups)
- 4 ounces (about 2 cups) sugar snap peas, thinly sliced on the diagonal
- 1 teaspoon poppy seeds
- 1 teaspoon sesame seeds

1. To make the vinaigrette, combine sugar, olive oil, vinegar, mustard, Worcestershire sauce, shallot, paprika, and salt in the jar of a blender or in the bowl of a food processor, and blend until smooth. Pour the dressing into a jar or serving container and chill until ready to serve.

2. Spray a piece of aluminum foil with nonstick cooking spray and set aside. To make the candied almonds, combine slivered almonds, sugar, and salt in a small skillet, and cook over medium heat, stirring often, until sugar is melted and almonds are coated and golden. This should take less than 5 minutes. Pour the candied almonds onto the foil, allow to cool completely, and then break into small chunks.

3. To assemble the salad, put the spinach in a bowl, and top with avocado, scallions, radishes, strawberries, snap peas, and candied almonds. Pour dressing over salad, sprinkle with poppy seeds and sesame seeds, toss, and serve immediately.

Note

Raspberry vinegar is very fruity with a sweet, unmistakable raspberry flavor. If you can't find it at your local grocery store, you can use balsamic vinegar in the dressing instead.

Spring Ham & Gruyère Quiche with Shaved Asparagus

I never appreciated quiche growing up, but now it's one of my favorite things to eat. If I see it on a breakfast, brunch, or dinner menu, I can't resist it. Paired with a big salad or a muffin (or a big salad AND a muffin!), I think it's such a dreamy meal. This recipe is based on the quiche my mom has made for as long as I can remember, the one that first taught me to love quiche. It has a really simple, buttery crust that you can just press into the pie pan, and an easy, savory filling that is customizable. It's great for serving to company, but also wonderful for a simple brunch or dinner at home. **Serves 6 to 8**

For the crust

- 1/2 cup butter, softened
- 3 ounces cream cheese, softened
- 1 cup all-purpose flour
- A pinch of salt

For the filling

- 4 eggs
- 1 (12-ounce) can evaporated milk
- 3/4 teaspoon salt
- 1/4 teaspoon granulated sugar
- Freshly ground black pepper
- 4 ounces finely diced ham (about 3/4 cup)
- 1/2 cup grated Gruyère cheese
- 1/4 cup finely diced scallions (3 to 4 scallions)
- 2 thick asparagus spears
- Freshly snipped chives for topping

continued

1. Preheat oven to 350°F and place a baking sheet on the middle rack.

2. In a large bowl or in the bowl of a stand mixer, beat the butter and cream cheese until smooth. Add flour and salt and mix just until combined. With lightly floured fingers, press the dough into the bottom and up the sides of a standard pie dish. I don't do this all at once. I basically build the sides first and then use what's left to fill in the bottom. Use a fork with the tines dipped in flour to press decorative lines into the edge of the crust.

3. In a medium bowl with high sides (like a large, glass measuring cup), beat the eggs, evaporated milk, salt, sugar, and pepper until smooth. Pour the mixture into the pie plate. Sprinkle ham, cheese, and scallions evenly over the surface then use the back of a spoon to gently push them under the liquid mixture so that they aren't floating on top.

4. Using a vegetable peeler, shave short sections of asparagus onto the top of the quiche. I hold the flat, woody end of the asparagus and shave off ribbons that are about 3 inches long. You have to be gentle or you'll snap the asparagus, which isn't a huge deal, but can be a little startling. Gently push the asparagus ribbons down with the back of a spoon. They don't need to be submerged under the egg mixture, but you don't want them sticking up into the air.

5. Place the quiche on the preheated baking sheet in the oven, and bake for 40-50 minutes until golden on top and set. If you gently jiggle the pie pan, it should not jiggle in the middle, and if you insert a paring knife in the center, it should come out wet but the liquid should be clear and not milky. Allow to cool 5-10 minutes before serving. Serve topped with fresh chives.

Note

Baking the quiche on a preheated baking sheet or pizza stone helps the bottom of the crust bake through evenly.

Strawberry & Hazelnut Croissant Sandwiches

These fantastic brunch sandwiches are really more than the sum of their parts, which are already delicious: juicy strawberries fresh from the garden, chocolatey hazelnut spread, and flaky, buttery croissants. They are so simple you almost don't need a recipe for them, and at the same time insanely delicious and a little bit fancy. I first had them at a ladies' brunch over a decade ago and have been making them regularly since. In the spring and summer, when backyard or farm-fresh strawberries are at their finest, these special sandwiches are perfect for a weekend breakfast or brunch, or even a sunny-afternoon snack.

Makes 8 large sandwiches

8 large croissants

Chocolate-hazelnut spread

2 pounds fresh strawberries, thinly sliced (about 6 cups)

Cut the croissants open. Spread a thin layer of hazelnut spread on the bottom half of each open croissant. Divide the strawberry slices evenly among the sandwiches. Put the tops on the croissants. Enjoy immediately.

Apricot & Sage Pork Tenderloin

Pork tenderloin is one of those main courses I forget exists, and then I make it and can't believe it isn't on the menu every single week. It is supremely easy to make: this recipe calls for a quick sear in a skillet then a quick oven-roast. And the pan sauce, with flavors of apricot, mustard, and sage, is tangy and sweet, and makes this entrée weekend worthy. ***Serves 6 to 8***

2 (1- to 1½-pound each) pork tenderloins

1 teaspoon kosher salt

Freshly ground black pepper

Extra virgin olive oil

¼ cup finely chopped shallots

1 cup chicken broth

6 fresh sage leaves

¼ cup apricot preserves

¼ cup apple cider vinegar

1 tablespoon stone-ground Dijon mustard

1 tablespoon butter

1. Preheat oven to 400°F.

2. Pat the tenderloins dry with paper towels, and season all over with salt and pepper. Heat 2 tablespoons olive oil in a large skillet over medium-high heat until shimmering. Add the tenderloins and cook without moving until brown on the bottom, 3–5 minutes. Turn the tenderloins over and continue cooking 2–3 more minutes until the other side is browned. Turn both tenderloins on their sides (I prop them up against each other), to allow the sides that are still white to brown; flip and repeat with the remaining side.

3. Remove the skillet from heat, transfer the tenderloins to a rimmed baking sheet, and roast until the pork reaches an internal temperature of 150°F, anywhere from 10–20 minutes depending on the size of

the tenderloins. Remove from the oven, place a large piece of heavy-duty aluminum foil over the top, and allow to rest while you make the pan sauce, about 10 minutes. Be sure to gently tuck the foil around the meat—it doesn't have to be tightly crimped.

4. Place the skillet over medium heat. If it looks completely dry, add another tablespoon of olive oil. Add the shallots and sauté until tender, 3–5 minutes. Add chicken broth and sage leaves, and bring to a simmer. Allow the broth to simmer for 3–4 minutes, scraping any browned bits of pork off the bottom of the skillet, until the liquid has reduced significantly. Add apricot preserves, vinegar, and mustard, and continue simmering 2–3 minutes until the sauce thickens slightly. Remove from heat, add butter, and remove sage leaves. Give the sauce a good whisk to incorporate the melted butter.

5. Slice the pork tenderloins into 1/2-inch-thick slices, and serve with sauce drizzled on top.

Honey-Roasted Carrots

Carrots are so delicious and so versatile. But I think a lot of times, they're a complete afterthought of a side dish. Boiled or steamed carrots with salt, pepper, and butter are just fine, but with just a tiny bit of effort, carrots can be so much more than just fine! This carrot recipe is super simple: you just mix up a quick sauce, pour it over the carrots, and pop them in the oven to roast. But it produces some seriously delicious carrots that are way better than boring. They're easy enough for a weeknight, but fancy enough for Sunday dinner or a springtime special occasion like Easter. **Serves 4**

1/4 cup butter

2 tablespoons honey

1 tablespoon apple juice

1/2 teaspoon salt

1/4 teaspoon nutmeg

1/4 teaspoon garlic powder

Freshly ground black pepper

1 pound (12 to 16) baby carrots, tops trimmed to about 1 inch

Minced fresh parsley

1. Preheat oven to 375°F.

2. In a small saucepan, combine butter, honey, apple juice, salt, nutmeg, garlic powder, and pepper over medium heat until the butter is melted.

3. Place the carrots on a rimmed baking sheet, pour the honey sauce over the carrots, and toss gently to coat.

4. Roast the carrots for 20 minutes. Top with parsley. Serve hot.

Note

If you can't find baby carrots, you can use baby-cut carrots instead. Baby carrots and baby-cut carrots are two different things. Baby carrots are those cute, mini carrots with lush, green tops on them, while baby-cut carrots are the prepeeled, precut carrots you buy in bags in the produce section.

Cheesy Biscuit–Topped Chicken Pot Pie

I think chicken pot pie is one of the ultimate comfort foods. If I'm having a bad day, chicken pot pie is the perfect dinner. If it's chilly outside, chicken pot pie comes to the rescue. Even my pickiest eaters love chicken pot pie, and this one, topped with cheesy biscuits and garlic butter, is just about as homey and delicious as it gets. This recipe makes a lot, so invite some friends over on a brisk spring evening and serve up bowls of biscuit-topped comfort! **Serves 8 to 10**

For the filling

3 cups diced cooked chicken breast (rotisserie chicken works great)

1 cup diced carrots

1/2 cup diced celery

1/2 pound small, waxy potatoes (about 12 to 14 baby or mini potatoes), diced

1 teaspoon salt, divided

1/3 cup butter

1/3 cup diced onion

2 cloves garlic, minced

1/3 cup all-purpose flour

1/2 teaspoon poultry seasoning

Freshly ground black pepper

1 (14.5-ounce) can chicken broth

2/3 cup whole milk

1 cup frozen peas

For the cheesy biscuits

2 cups all-purpose flour

2 1/2 teaspoons baking powder

1/2 teaspoon salt

6 tablespoons cold butter, cut into pieces

3/4 cup buttermilk

1/2 cup grated cheddar cheese

4 tablespoons butter

1 teaspoon minced fresh parsley

1/2 teaspoon garlic powder

continued

1. Preheat oven to 425°F.

2. Place the chicken in a 9 x 9-inch or 7 x 11-inch baking dish.

3. Put the carrots, celery, and potatoes in a medium pot with $1/2$ teaspoon salt, cover with water, and bring to a boil over high heat. Cook for 10–15 minutes until tender. Drain and add to the pan with the chicken.

4. In the same pot, melt the butter over medium heat. Add onion and garlic and cook until tender, about 5 minutes. Add the flour, remaining salt, poultry seasoning, and pepper, and cook, whisking steadily, for 1–2 minutes. Add the broth and milk and cook, whisking steadily, until thickened, 3–5 minutes. Taste and adjust with additional salt and pepper if needed.

5. Pour the sauce over the chicken and vegetables, add the peas, and stir gently. Bake for 15 minutes while you make the cheddar biscuits.

6. In the bowl of a food processor, combine flour, baking powder, and salt. Add butter pieces and pulse about 10 times. Add the buttermilk and cheese, and pulse until the dough comes together in a ball.

7. When the chicken has baked for 15 minutes, put large spoonfuls of dough evenly over the top. Make sure the biscuits are no thicker than 1 inch or they won't bake all the way through in the middle. Bake another 15–20 minutes until the filling is bubbly and the biscuits are golden and baked all the way through.

8. Right before the chicken pot pie is finished baking, melt the 4 tablespoons butter. Mix with parsley and garlic powder. When the pot pie is golden on top, pull it out of the oven, and spoon or brush the garlic butter mixture over the biscuits. Serve hot.

Spring Parmesan Risotto

Risotto is one of those rare dishes that tastes comforting and homey, but seems incredibly indulgent—the very best of both worlds. It's creamy and luxurious, and in this case, full of fresh spring flavors. This recipe is perfect for a cozy evening meal after a trip to the farmer's market, or after a brisk afternoon spent harvesting peas and asparagus from the backyard garden. It is fancy enough to serve weekend guests, but so good you'll want to make it even when no one is visiting. It takes a little time and attention, but it isn't hard to make. In fact, if you find cooking relaxing, risotto is just about perfect. Put on some music, tie on an apron, and stir your cares away! **Serves 4 to 6**

2 (14.5-ounce) cans chicken or vegetable broth

1 cup water

1 tablespoon extra virgin olive oil

1 tablespoon butter

1/2 cup finely chopped leek, white and light green parts only, (about 1 medium leek)

1 1/2 cups Arborio rice

1 clove garlic, minced or grated

1/2 bunch asparagus, chopped into 1/2-inch pieces

1/2 cup fresh garden peas

A splash of white wine

1/2 cup shredded Parmesan cheese, plus extra for serving

1/4 cup finely snipped fresh chives, plus extra for serving

1 tablespoon finely minced fresh parsley

Salt

Freshly ground black pepper

continued

1. Combine broth and water in a medium saucepan and bring to a simmer. Once simmering, turn the heat down but not off. The broth needs to stay hot.

2. Combine olive oil and butter in a large pan or skillet over medium heat. Add leeks and sauté, stirring frequently, until leeks are tender, about 5 minutes. Add rice and garlic and sauté, stirring frequently, about 2 more minutes.

3. Reduce heat to medium low. Add $1/2$ cup hot liquid to the rice, and stir slowly but constantly, until the liquid is absorbed. Repeat, adding liquid, $1/2$ cup at a time, and stirring until it is absorbed, until all the liquid has been added. This should take about 25 minutes.

4. Add asparagus, peas, and a splash of white wine and sauté, stirring constantly, until the liquid is mostly absorbed. Taste a few grains of rice to check the texture. If they're still noticeably crunchy inside, repeat step 3 using just hot water until the rice is creamy and just al dente. You don't want the finished risotto to be dry or mushy.

5. Add Parmesan cheese, chives, and parsley and stir to combine. Salt and pepper to taste. Serve immediately with extra Parmesan and chives for sprinkling on top.

Notes

1. In a pinch, you can use any short- or medium-grain rice in place of the Arborio rice. I've used Calrose before and it was delicious.

2. Since fresh garden peas aren't available for most of the year, you can use frozen peas in their place. Because they cook so quickly and are added close to but not at the very end of the recipe, you can just add them frozen.

3. The texture of risotto is creamy, but not dry, and the rice should be tender, but not mushy. The nice thing about risotto is that if you get to the point where you've added all your liquid, and the rice is still crunchy, you can just add more hot water in $1/2$-cup increments until the texture is right.

New Potatoes & Peas in Cream Sauce

New potatoes and fresh garden peas covered in a savory cream sauce is basically the most comforting, homey dish I can imagine. It's farm food at its finest—simple, filling, and full of flavor. It's the kind of old-fashioned favorite that everyone's grandma has some version of. We love shelling plump, green peas and digging new potatoes out of our garden so that we can make this side dish for late springtime dinners. **Serves 6**

1 pound new potatoes (about 32 small, single-bite potatoes)

Salt

1 cup shelled fresh garden peas

3 tablespoons butter

1/4 cup finely chopped onion

3 tablespoons all-purpose flour

1 1/2 cups whole milk

1/2 teaspoon chicken bouillon

1/4 teaspoon salt

Freshly ground black pepper

1. Put the potatoes in a medium saucepan. Add enough water to cover the potatoes by 1 inch. Add a very large pinch of salt to the water, and bring it to a boil over high heat. Cook until the potatoes are tender, 10–15 minutes. Add the peas to the pot and continue cooking for 1–2 minutes more, until both peas and potatoes are tender. Drain the water out of the pot and set aside until the sauce is ready.

2. While the potatoes are cooking, make the cream sauce. In a small saucepan, melt the butter over medium heat. Add the onion and sauté until translucent, about 5 minutes. Add the flour and whisk vigorously to make sure there are no lumps. Cook the flour and butter mixture for 1 minute. Whisk in the

milk and stir constantly until the sauce thickens. Whisk in the chicken bouillon, salt, and pepper.

3. Pour the sauce over the peas and potatoes, salt and pepper to taste, and serve immediately.

Notes

1. New potatoes have a tender skin that hasn't cured yet. They are really fresh, having just been dug up. You can find them in your vegetable garden or at the farmer's market, but probably not at a regular grocery store. In their place, you can use the smallest baby potatoes you can find, ideally single-bite potatoes.

2. Frozen peas will definitely work in place of the fresh peas. Add them to the potato pot after the first 7 minutes of cooking.

Cherry Crumb Cake

Cherries are among the first fruits to ripen every year, and after a winter of frozen and canned fruits, we welcome them with open arms. We have a few cherry trees in our yard and more at my husband's office, and we still can't resist buying a basket of cherries at the farmstand if they look especially beautiful; cherries are just too pretty and too tasty to pass by. I love eating them fresh, but they also make baked goods like this lightly spiced crumb cake extra special.

Serves 12 to 16

For the streusel

1 cup all-purpose flour

$1/2$ cup granulated sugar

$1/2$ cup brown sugar

$1/2$ teaspoon cinnamon

$1/4$ teaspoon cardamom

$1/8$ teaspoon salt

$1/2$ cup butter, melted

$1/2$ teaspoon vanilla extract

For the cake

$1/2$ cup butter, softened

$1 1/2$ cups granulated sugar

2 eggs

1 cup sour cream

1 teaspoon vanilla extract

2 cups all-purpose flour

1 teaspoon baking powder

$1/2$ teaspoon baking soda

$1/2$ teaspoon salt

3 cups cherries, pitted and halved

For the glaze

1 cup powdered sugar

5 tablespoons heavy cream

$1/4$ teaspoon vanilla extract

A pinch of salt

continued

1. Preheat oven to 350°F. Spray a 9 x 13-inch baking pan with nonstick cooking spray and set aside.

2. To make the streusel, combine the flour, granulated sugar, brown sugar, spices, and salt in a medium bowl until well mixed. Add the melted butter and vanilla, and stir until combined. Set aside.

3. To make the cake, beat butter and sugar in a large bowl on medium speed until light and fluffy, about 2 minutes. Add eggs, 1 at a time, beating and scraping down the sides of the bowl with each addition. Add sour cream and vanilla, and beat until smooth.

4. In a medium bowl, combine flour, baking powder, baking soda, and salt. Add flour mixture to wet ingredients and beat on low speed until just combined.

5. Spread about 2/3 of the batter in the bottom of the baking pan. Spread the cherry halves evenly over the batter. Crumble the streusel mixture with your hands, and sprinkle half of it over the cherries. Spoon the remaining cake batter over the streusel then top with the remaining streusel crumbles.

6. Bake for 40–45 minutes, until a toothpick inserted in the center of the cake comes out clean.

7. Allow the cake to cool completely.

8. While the cake cools, prepare the glaze. Combine all the glaze ingredients in a medium bowl and whisk until smooth. If the glaze is too thick to drizzle, whisk in a little more cream until a drizzleable consistency is achieved. Drizzle the glaze over the cooled cake. Cut and serve.

Notes & Variations

1. If fresh cherries aren't in season, you can use 2 (14.5-ounce) cans of cherries instead. These whole, pitted cherries are packed in water and are usually found on the canned fruit aisle of the grocery store. This is NOT canned pie filling! Use them as you would fresh cherries, draining them and cutting them in half. You can also use frozen cherries, just be sure to thaw them first.

2. When sour pie cherries are in season, use them in place of the sweet cherries. You can also find these canned. The packaging usually says something along the lines of "Red Tart Cherries."

3. In the summertime, try using raspberries in place of the cherries!

Classic Carrot Cake with Cream Cheese Frosting

I'm not exactly picky when it comes to carrot cake (I'll eat it even if it's too dry or, more often than not, too moist), but I think this recipe is perfection—lightly spiced, chock-full of not only carrots, but also plump golden raisins, tangy bits of pineapple, and sweet coconut flakes, and topped with rich cream cheese frosting. It's dense without being stodgy, and moist without being soggy. Truly a rustic and wonderful gem of a cake. **Serves 12 to 16**

For the cake

- 4 eggs
- 2 cups granulated sugar
- 3/4 cup vegetable or canola oil
- 2 1/2 cups all-purpose flour
- 2 teaspoons cinnamon
- 1 teaspoon baking soda
- 1 teaspoon baking powder
- 1 teaspoon salt
- 2 cups shredded carrots (about 8 ounces)
- 1 (8-ounce) can crushed pineapple, drained
- 1 cup golden raisins
- 1 cup sweetened coconut flakes

For the cream cheese frosting

- 1 (8-ounce) brick cream cheese, softened
- 1/2 cup butter, softened
- 1 pound (about 3 3/4 cups) powdered sugar
- 1 teaspoon vanilla
- A pinch of salt
- 1 cup chopped pecans for topping

continued

1. Preheat oven to 350°F. Spray a 9 x 13-inch baking pan with nonstick cooking spray.

2. In a large bowl or in the bowl of a stand mixer, combine eggs, sugar, and oil.

3. In a medium bowl, combine flour, cinnamon, baking soda, baking powder, and salt. Add the dry ingredients to the large bowl, and stir until just combined. Add the carrots, pineapple, raisins, and coconut, and stir until they're evenly distributed.

4. Spread the batter in the prepared pan, and bake 40–45 minutes, until a toothpick inserted in the center of the cake comes out clean. Allow the cake to cool completely before frosting.

5. While the cake cools, make the frosting. In a large bowl or in the bowl of a stand mixer, beat the cream cheese and butter until smooth. Add the powdered sugar, vanilla, and salt, and beat until smooth. When the cake is completely cool, frost it, sprinkle with chopped pecans if desired, and serve.

Note

Don't use preshredded carrots from the grocery store. They're cut too thickly.

Double-Citrus Poppy Seed Cake

I love this cake because even though cake is by nature fancy, this one feels very casual, like you just threw it together. I think it has something to do with its manageable size and lack of frosting on the sides! Its bright, sunny citrus flavors bring some sunshine to what might be otherwise gloomy early spring weekends. And I won't tell anyone if you have it for an afternoon snack or even breakfast.

Serves 8

For the cake

1 ruby red grapefruit, zested

1 large sweet orange, zested

1 cup granulated sugar

1/2 cup butter, softened

2 eggs

1/2 teaspoon vanilla extract

1/2 teaspoon orange extract

1 1/2 cups all-purpose flour

2 teaspoons baking powder

1/2 teaspoon salt

2/3 cup buttermilk

2 teaspoons poppy seeds

For the citrus cream cheese frosting

3 ounces cream cheese, softened

3 tablespoons butter, softened

1 1/2 cups powdered sugar

Remaining zest from the cake (about 1 teaspoon)

1/4 teaspoon vanilla extract

A pinch of salt

continued

1. Preheat oven to 350°F. Butter and flour an 8-inch round cake pan, or spray with nonstick baking spray with flour.

2. In a small bowl, combine grapefruit and orange zest. Mix well.

3. In a large bowl, combine sugar and half of the zest mixture (about 1 table-spoon). Set the remaining zest aside for the frosting. Rub the sugar and zest together with your fingers until the sugar becomes really fragrant and the consistency of wet sand. Add butter and beat on medium speed until light and fluffy, about 1 minute. Add eggs, vanilla, and orange extract and beat until smooth.

4. In a small bowl, combine flour, baking powder, and salt. Add half of the dry ingredients to the large mixing bowl and beat just until combined then follow with half of the buttermilk. Repeat, and then gently fold in the poppy seeds.

5. Pour batter into the prepared pan, and bake for 35–38 minutes until the top of the cake is golden and springs back when touched, or a toothpick poked into the middle of the cake comes out clean.

6. Let the cake cool in the pan for 10 minutes before carefully turning out onto a wire rack. Let it cool completely before frosting.

7. When the cake is completely cool, make the frosting. In a large bowl or in the bowl of a stand mixer, beat cream cheese and butter until smooth. Add powdered sugar, remaining citrus zest, vanilla, and salt, and beat until smooth. Spread the frosting on the top of the cake only. Slice and serve.

Notes & Variations

1. Feel free to experiment with the citrus in this cake! Mix it up and see what your favorite combinations are.

2. Leftovers of this cake need to be stored in the fridge, but because the cake is made with butter, it really tastes best at room temperature. So do both: store leftovers tightly covered in the fridge, but let them come to room temperature before serving.

Strawberry-Rhubarb Crumble

Is it even spring if you don't eat a strawberry-rhubarb baked good? This delicious dessert, topped with big, toothsome chunks of sweet, cinnamon-scented oatmeal crumble, is one of my favorites. The high ratio of strawberries to rhubarb makes sure the filling stays a gorgeous shade of red and keeps it from being too tart. It's amazing topped with vanilla ice cream or sweetened whipped cream. Or both.

Serves 8

For the crumble topping

- 1 cup all-purpose flour
- 1/2 cup old-fashioned rolled oats
- 1/3 cup granulated sugar
- 1/3 cup brown sugar
- 1/2 teaspoon baking powder
- 1/2 teaspoon cinnamon
- 1/4 teaspoon salt
- 1/2 cup butter, melted

For the filling

- 2 pounds strawberries, chopped (about 6 cups chopped strawberries)
- 1/2 pound rhubarb, chopped (about 1 1/2 cups chopped rhubarb)
- 1/2 cup granulated sugar
- 3 tablespoons cornstarch
- 1 tablespoon fresh lemon juice
- A pinch of salt

continued

1. Preheat oven to 375°F. Line a rimmed baking sheet with aluminum foil and set aside.

2. In a medium bowl, combine all crumble ingredients except butter. Stir until well mixed. Add butter and stir until evenly mixed; set aside.

3. To make the filling, combine all ingredients in a large bowl, and let sit for 10 minutes. After the filling has rested, stir it gently, then pour it into a deep 9-inch pie pan or 8-inch square baking dish.

4. Break the crumble topping up into chunks with a fork or with your hands. Spread the topping evenly over the fruit, going all the way to the edges of the pie pan.

5. Place the pie pan on the foil-lined baking sheet, and bake for 35–45 minutes, until the fruit is bubbling and the topping is golden brown on top. Remove from the oven and allow to cool slightly before eating. Serve warm, topped with whipped cream or vanilla ice cream.

Two-Layer Fresh Strawberry Pie

Fresh strawberries are one of life's simple pleasures. They taste and smell just like candy, and they return year after year all by themselves. I remember a family road trip to the Pacific Northwest when I was a kid. It happened during the summer (as most of our road trips did), and every restaurant had some version of strawberry pie on the menu. I think that trip made me believe strawberry pie was the most beautiful, delicious, extraordinary dessert ever, and I haven't changed my mind yet! **Makes 6 to 8 servings**

For the crust

- 1 1/4 cups all-purpose flour
- 1 1/2 teaspoons granulated sugar
- 1/2 teaspoon salt
- 6 tablespoons cold butter, cut into chunks
- 4 tablespoons cold shortening, cut into chunks
- 1/2 cup ice water (you won't use all of it)

For the strawberry layer

- 1/2 cup granulated sugar
- 1 tablespoon cornstarch
- 1 1/2 pounds fresh strawberries, coarsely chopped (about 4 1/2 cups chopped strawberries)

- 1 1/2 ounces strawberry Jell-O (half of a small box)
- 1 1/2 teaspoons fresh lemon juice
- 1 teaspoon butter
- Lightly sweetened whipped cream for serving

For the cream cheese layer

- 1/2 cup heavy whipping cream
- 1/3 cup granulated sugar
- 1 (8-ounce) brick cream cheese, cut into chunks and softened
- 1/2 teaspoon vanilla extract

continued

1. To prepare the crust, combine flour, sugar, and salt in the bowl of a food processor. Pulse a few times to combine. Add the chunks of butter and shortening, and pulse until the mixture resembles coarse corn meal, with a few chunks about the size of peas remaining. Measure out $1/4$ cup cold water, add it to the food processor, and pulse until the mixture begins to come together in a single ball of dough. If the dough is still a bit dry, add a small amount more water. Remove the dough from the food processor. Shape it into a disk about 1 inch thick, and wrap it in plastic wrap. Refrigerate it for 45 minutes to 1 hour.

2. Unwrap the chilled dough and place it on a floured work surface. Roll it out into a circle about $1/8$ inch thick. Carefully transfer the dough to a 9-inch pie plate. Without stretching the dough, press it into the bottom and up the sides of the pie plate. Using a sharp paring knife or a pair of kitchen shears, trim off any extra dough that hangs over the edge of the pie plate by more than 1 inch.

Fold the extra inch of dough under itself so that the pie crust is thick on the edge and comes just to the edge of the pie plate. Use the tines of a fork to press a decorative pattern into the edge of the crust. Prick the bottom and sides of the crust with a fork, and freeze 15 minutes.

3. Preheat oven to 425°F. Gently line the chilled crust with aluminum foil, making sure it is pressed right up against the bottom and sides of the crust. Fill the foil with pie weights or dried beans or rice. Bake the crust for 15 minutes. Remove the crust from the oven, and reduce the oven heat to 375°F. Carefully lift the foil out and set it aside, and continue baking the empty, unlined crust for 10–15 more minutes until it is golden brown. Cool completely before filling.

4. To make the strawberry layer, mix sugar and cornstarch in a saucepan. Mash $1/2$ cup of the berries and add enough water to make 1 cup of liquid. Stir into the sugar mixture. Cook over medium heat until boiling, stirring constantly. Boil 2 minutes. Remove from heat and whisk in

Jell-O, lemon juice, and butter. Stir until the Jell-O is dissolved then allow to cool for about 30 minutes.

5. To make the cream cheese layer, beat cream and sugar in a medium bowl until stiff peaks form. With the mixer on low, add softened cream cheese, little by little, and beat until smooth. Beat in the vanilla. Spoon into the pie crust and smooth the top.

6. Arrange the reserved strawberries decoratively on top of the cream cheese layer. Pour the cooled glaze over the top. Chill until the glaze is set, 1–2 hours. Serve with sweetened whipped cream.

Notes

1. If you are using homegrown or farm-fresh berries, they are probably much smaller than the ones you can get at the grocery store. You can halve them if they're medium size, and leave them whole if they're tiny.

2. The strawberry layer in this pie is based on a recipe from my friend, Anne Cropper. Thanks for sharing such a delicious strawberry treat with the world, Anne!

3. Here's a bonus recipe! When you make homemade pie crust for a pie, you inevitably have some scraps of pie crust leftover. Make pie crust cookies! They're a favorite in our family. Lay the pie crust scraps on a baking sheet and sprinkle generously with cinnamon sugar. Bake at whatever temperature your regular pie crust should bake at just until golden. Cool slightly before eating.

summer

SUMMER AT THE FARMHOUSE is bursting with life! The flower beds are overflowing with zinnias and dahlias and the heady smell of sweet peas. We pick buckets of berries for salads, snacks, jams, and desserts, although half the berries go straight from juice-stained hands to juice-stained mouths. The kitchen smells like candy after a morning spent making strawberry jam. We eat dinner outside at the patio table, dinners that try to keep up with all the garden has produced for the day—green beans and tomatoes, and giant zucchini that must have been hiding beneath vines and leaves. We run and swim and stay up late making bonfires and s'mores, enjoying every last drop of daylight. After the sun goes down, we open the windows and let the cool evening air fill the house, and we listen to the frogs and crickets sing us to sleep.

Farmhouse Weekends in Summer

make homemade jam • pick peaches • chase fireflies • have a picnic under a tree
• visit the farmers market • roast marshmallows over a bonfire
• harvest honey from beehives • cut flowers from a u-pick farm
• bake muffins with blueberries you picked yourself • bottle sour pie cherries
• have a clambake on the beach • sleep under the stars

Blackberry Skillet Cake with Whipped Cream

This rustic cake is such a wonderful treat for breakfast (or dessert). It's lightly scented with cinnamon and nutmeg, is full of juicy summer berries, and takes less time to prep than your oven takes to preheat. And it's so incredibly versatile! We usually throw in a few fistfuls of fresh blackberries from the backyard, but we've tried all kinds of summer fruits and never found a combination we didn't love.

Serves 6 to 8

$^1/_2$ cup butter

1 cup granulated sugar

1 cup all-purpose flour

1 teaspoon baking powder

$^1/_2$ teaspoon cinnamon

$^1/_4$ teaspoon nutmeg

$^1/_4$ teaspoon salt

1 cup whole milk

2 cups fresh blackberries

Lightly sweetened whipped cream

1. Place the butter in the bottom of a 10-inch cast iron skillet or Dutch oven and put it in the oven. Preheat oven to 375°F and allow the butter to melt while the oven is heating.

2. In a medium bowl, combine sugar, flour, baking powder, cinnamon, nutmeg, and salt. Whisk in milk until mostly smooth. When the butter has melted and the oven is up to temperature, pour the butter into the batter, whisk it until well combined, and pour the batter into the hot pan. Sprinkle the berries evenly over the top.

3. Bake for 30–35 minutes, until golden brown and baked through. Serve warm, topped with whipped cream.

continued

Notes & Variations

1. Your butter might melt before your oven is fully preheated. Keep an eye on the butter and pull the skillet out as soon as the butter is melted so that it doesn't burn. You can mix the butter into the batter as soon as it is melted, but wait to pour the batter into the skillet until the oven is up to temperature.

2. So many different fruits can be used in place of the blackberries in this easy and delicious dish. Try diced or thinly sliced peaches, plums, or apples, or any kind of berry in place of the blackberries.

3. You can also use frozen berries and enjoy this cake all year long, even in the fall, winter, and early spring. I find it's best to thaw the berries first so that you don't end up with cold spots in your batter.

4. Try topping with powdered sugar or cinnamon sugar instead of whipped cream. Serve it with vanilla ice cream for dessert.

5. If you don't have a 10-inch cast iron skillet or Dutch oven, you can use a 9-inch square baking pan and it should bake for the same amount of time.

Blueberry & Cream Cheese Breakfast Bake

Blueberries are one of the best-loved fruits at our house. The kids are always willing to run out to the garden to fill a bowl with sweet, ripe blueberries. While they are out there, they probably eat as many as they bring back to the kitchen. This weekend breakfast bake is an easy recipe that makes excellent (and extremely tasty) use of summer's fresh blueberries. Drizzled with maple syrup and sprinkled with powdered sugar, and studded with indigo berries and bits of tangy cream cheese, this dish would be at home on the menu of your favorite weekend brunch spot. But you can get it ready with just a few minutes of work before you go to bed, and then pop it in the oven while you shower and brush your teeth the next morning. **Serves 8**

1 1/2 pounds day-old croissants (10 to 11 large croissants)

6 eggs

1 1/2 cups whole milk

1/4 cup brown sugar

2 teaspoons vanilla extract

1/2 teaspoon salt

1 cup fresh blueberries

4 ounces cream cheese

Maple syrup and powdered sugar for serving

1. Tear the croissants into large chunks (3 to 4 large chunks per croissant is fine) and place on a large rimmed baking sheet.

2. In a medium bowl, whisk eggs, milk, brown sugar, vanilla, and salt until well mixed. Drizzle the egg mixture over the croissant pieces and toss gently to coat. Allow the croissants to soak in the egg mixture for about 30 minutes, tossing occasionally to make sure the pieces are evenly coated.

continued

3. Spray a 9 x 13-inch baking dish with nonstick cooking spray. Arrange half of the croissant pieces in the bottom of the baking dish. Sprinkle half of the blueberries evenly over the top. Pinch off small chunks of cream cheese and tuck them evenly among the croissant pieces. Use about half of the cream cheese. Repeat the layers with the remaining croissant pieces, blueberries, and bits of cream cheese. If there is any egg mixture remaining in the bowl (if there's any, it won't be much), drizzle it over the top of the croissants. Cover with plastic wrap and refrigerate overnight.

4. In the morning, get the baking dish out of the fridge and leave it on the counter while the oven preheats to 350°F. Uncover and bake for 35–40 minutes or until the top of the croissants are nicely browned. Serve hot, topped with a drizzle of maple syrup and a sprinkle of powdered sugar.

Notes

1. If you have a little extra time in the morning (or don't have any time the night before), you can make this entire recipe in one go without the overnight stint in the fridge.

2. If you remember to, leave the croissants out on the counter all day to get stale and dry.

Cinnamon-Sugar Zucchini Bread

Zucchini is such a delight to grow in the backyard summer garden, and bless its heart, it gets out of control so quickly! I think it's because zucchini can so easily hide under those giant, green leaves, and go undetected until they're the size of baseball bats. Luckily, there are about a million ways to enjoy zucchini, and this cinnamon-sugar quick bread is one of my favorites. It makes a yummy addition to weekend brunch tables and afternoon snacks, and the double-chocolate variation is every bit as delicious as the original cinnamon sugar.

Makes 2 standard loaves

3 cups all-purpose flour

1 tablespoon cinnamon

1 teaspoon baking soda

1 teaspoon baking powder

1 teaspoon salt

3 eggs

2 cups granulated sugar

1 cup vegetable or canola oil

2 teaspoons vanilla extract

2 cups grated zucchini

1. Preheat oven to 325°F. Spray 2 standard loaf pans with nonstick cooking spray. Cut 2 pieces of parchment paper the same width as the bottom of the loaf pans and 10–12 inches longer. Line each pan with 1 of these strips of parchment paper so that the ends of the paper extend past the ends of the pan, and lightly spray again with nonstick cooking spray.

2. Combine flour, cinnamon, baking soda, baking powder, and salt in a medium bowl. In a large bowl, whisk eggs, sugar, oil, and vanilla until smooth. Add dry ingredients, stirring until just combined. Stir in zucchini and mix until it is well distributed.

3. Pour into prepared pans and bake for 60–65 minutes. Let cool in pan for 10 minutes, then remove using the parchment paper slings, and cool completely on wire racks.

Variations

1. For double-chocolate zucchini bread, decrease cinnamon to 1 teaspoon (or omit it entirely if you aren't a fan of chocolate and cinnamon together), add 5 tablespoons cocoa powder to dry ingredients, and stir in 1 cup mini chocolate chips before pouring into pans. Sprinkle more mini chocolate chips on top and bake.

2. For an extra boost of cinnamon goodness, brush the tops of the warm loaves with melted butter while they're still hot, and sprinkle with a mixture of 4 teaspoons sugar and $1/2$ teaspoon cinnamon.

Peach Crumb Muffins

I remember eating a peach muffin on vacation when I was younger. I'm not sure it was my first time eating a peach muffin, but it's my earliest memory of eating one, and it obviously made an impression. It was tender and flavorful, full of tiny bits of juicy summer peach, and topped with a lightly spiced crumb topping. This recipe makes muffins with all those same characteristics: fluffy, delicious, and peachy, with a lip-smacking, buttery cinnamon-brown sugar topping. They're so good, it's hard to limit yourself to just one! **Makes 18 muffins**

For the crumb topping

1/2 cup all-purpose flour

1/4 cup granulated sugar

1/4 cup brown sugar

1/4 teaspoon cinnamon

A pinch of salt

1/4 cup butter, melted

For the muffins

2 1/2 cups all-purpose flour

1 cup granulated sugar

1 tablespoon baking powder

1 teaspoon baking soda

1/2 teaspoon salt

1/8 teaspoon nutmeg

1 cup buttermilk

2 eggs

2 teaspoons vanilla extract

1/2 cup butter, melted

1 1/2 cups finely chopped fresh peaches

continued

1. Preheat oven to 375°F. Generously spray 18 muffin cups with nonstick baking spray, being sure to get the top of the pan as well. You can also line the pans with cupcake papers.

2. To make the crumb topping, combine flour, granulated sugar, brown sugar, cinnamon, and salt in a medium bowl. Add the melted butter, and stir to combine. Set aside.

3. To make the muffins, combine flour, sugar, baking powder, baking soda, salt, and nutmeg in a large bowl.

4. In a medium bowl or in a large glass measuring cup, combine buttermilk, eggs, and vanilla, stirring until well mixed. Add the buttermilk mixture to the dry ingredients and stir gently until mostly combined. Add the melted butter and stir just until smooth.

5. Gently fold the chopped peaches into the muffin batter.

6. Divide the batter evenly among the 18 muffins cups. You will use all the batter, which means the cups will be filled almost to the top. Sprinkle the crumb topping evenly on top of the muffins.

7. Bake for 15–18 minutes, until golden on the edges, and until a skewer inserted in the middle of a muffin comes out clean. Allow to cool in the pan for 5–10 minutes then gently remove the muffins from the pan and set them on a wire rack to cool completely.

Notes

1. If you have a small 6-muffin pan, and a regular 12-muffin pan, the two together will work perfectly. If you only have 12-muffin pans, spray 2 full pans, and only use 18 of the cups. Fill the 6 empty cups with water to help the muffins bake evenly.

2. These muffins are best fresh, but they're actually quite good leftover, too. Store any leftovers in an airtight container and eat them within 2 days of baking.

3. If fresh peaches aren't in season, you can use frozen or even canned peaches instead, although canned peaches won't be as flavorful. Allow frozen peach to thaw before adding them to the batter.

Strawberry Fields Salad with Mixed Greens, Sugared Pecans & Feta

A few years ago, my husband's siblings all got together to throw his parents a 50th wedding anniversary party in Pismo Beach, CA. We thought it would be a fun homage to the quarter of a century they spent in the Central Valley to have the caterers serve Santa Maria Barbecue. I know they had all the basics and that everything was delicious, but mostly I just remember this salad! The combination of flavors is bright, fresh, and absolutely delicious. We eat this a lot, and I love buying and preparing extras of the ingredients so that I can quickly throw them together for lunch for a few days after. It is especially wonderful during the spring and summer, when you can use locally grown greens and red, sun-ripened berries from your backyard. **Makes 8 to 10 servings**

For the sugared pecans

1 egg white

1 tablespoon water

1 pound (about 4 cups) pecan halves

1 cup granulated sugar

3/4 teaspoon salt

For the red wine vinaigrette

1/2 cup extra virgin olive oil

5 tablespoons granulated sugar

1/4 cup red wine vinegar

1/4 cup water

1 tablespoon freshly squeezed lemon juice

1/2 teaspoon salt

1 clove garlic

Freshly ground black pepper

For the salad

1 (10-ounce) package mixed spring greens (or a 50/50 blend of spring greens and baby spinach)

1 pound fresh strawberries, sliced (about 3 cups)

5 ounces dried, tart cherries (about 1 cup)

Sugared Pecans

1/2 large red onion, very thinly sliced

3 ounces crumbled feta cheese

Red Wine Vinaigrette

continued

1. To make the sugared pecans, begin by preheating oven to 250°F. In a large, plastic container with a tight-fitting lid, combine egg white and water with a fork until frothy. Add the pecan halves, put the lid on tightly, and shake until the pecans are coated in liquid.

2. In a small bowl, combine sugar and salt. Pour the sugar mixture onto the pecans, put the lid on again, and shake until the pecans are evenly and completely coated with sugar.

3. Line a rimmed baking sheet with parchment paper. Pour the pecans onto the baking sheet in a single, even layer. Bake for 1 hour, stirring gently every 20 minutes.

4. Remove the pecans from the oven and allow to cool slightly. Taste a few nuts (blow on them first so you don't burn your mouth!), and if they are not completely crunchy and delicious, put them back in the oven for another 20 minutes.

5. Allow the pecans to cool completely before using.

6. To make the vinaigrette, combine all ingredients in a blender or in the bowl of a food processor, and blend until smooth, 20–30 seconds. Chill until needed.

7. To assemble the salad, layer greens, strawberries, dried cherries, pecans, red onion, and crumbled feta in a large serving bowl in that order. It looks really lovely before you toss it, so wait until the last second to do that, or let guests toss it as they serve themselves.

8. Pour the vinaigrette into a smaller pitcher and allow people to dress their salad to taste.

Note

I won't say the sugared pecans are the best part of the salad because all the different components of this recipe work together in a beautiful, synergistic symphony of flavor. But they really are the best part! I always make the full recipe, which is way more sugared pecans than I need for a single salad, because we tend to snack on them a lot while they're cooling. Also, they make a great holiday gift for friends and neighbors! If you wish, you can add 1 teaspoon of cinnamon to the sugar and salt mixture to make pecans for holiday gifting.

White Cheddar & Zucchini Egg Bites

This might become one of your go-to summer recipes, especially if you're like me and grow more zucchini than you know what to do with! These savory, cheese-stuffed egg bites are like mini frittatas—light, tasty, and full of herby garden flavor. They are super simple to make and can be served basically any time of day. They are delicious for breakfast and brunch, make a fantastic, quick lunch, and can even be the star of a meatless dinner after a trip to the farmer's market. And their diminutive size makes them as cute as they are delectable.

Makes 12 egg bites or 4 to 6 servings

1 tablespoon extra virgin olive oil

1 cup firmly packed grated zucchini (from about 1 medium zucchini, about 6 ounces)

2 scallions, minced, white and light green parts only

1 teaspoon minced fresh thyme

8 eggs

1 heaping cup grated sharp white cheddar cheese (about 4 ounces), plus extra for sprinkling on top

1/2 cup cottage cheese

1/2 teaspoon salt

Freshly ground black pepper

1. Preheat oven to 350°F. Spray a 12-cup muffin pan with nonstick baking spray. If you have a silicone muffin pan, that's even better.

2. In a medium skillet, heat olive oil over medium heat. Sauté zucchini and scallions until tender and until any extra liquid from the zucchini has evaporated, 5–6 minutes. You don't want the zucchini to start sticking to the pan or browning. Remove from heat and stir in fresh thyme. Divide the zucchini mixture evenly among the muffin pan cups.

3. In the jar of a blender, combine eggs, cheddar cheese, cottage cheese, salt, and pepper. Blend until completely

smooth. Pour the egg mixture over the zucchini in the muffin pan. Sprinkle a little bit of the reserved cheddar cheese on top of each egg bite then add an extra pinch of freshly ground black pepper on top.

4. Bake for 20-23 minutes until puffy and golden. Allow them to cool in the pan for 5 minutes before removing. Serve immediately.

Note

These are even better on day 2! You can reheat them in the microwave for 1 minute.

Homemade Hushpuppies

If you've never had hushpuppies, you've been missing out! They're little savory cornmeal donut holes, or tiny onion-flavored fritters. They're delicious, and the perfect accompaniment to seafood, BBQ, chili, and all Southern comfort foods. We love topping ours with honey butter or homemade jam. The mix of sweet and savory is out of this world. Don't let the frying scare you. Frying foods is easy, it just takes a little practice and a little patience. You'll need a thermometer for this recipe. **Makes about 2 dozen hushpuppies**

Canola or peanut oil (or your favorite frying oil)

Scant ³/4 cup cornmeal

Scant ³/4 cup all-purpose flour

2 tablespoons granulated sugar

¹/4 teaspoon baking soda

³/4 teaspoon salt

¹/2 cup buttermilk

2 tablespoons vegetable or canola oil

1 egg

¹/4 cup grated onion (about ¹/4 to ¹/2 large onion)

2 tablespoons snipped fresh chives

1. Pour about 2 inches of oil in a heavy-bottom pot or Dutch oven. Place it over medium heat and bring it to 350°F.

2. In a medium bowl, combine cornmeal, flour, sugar, baking soda, and salt.

3. In a small bowl or small glass measuring cup, combine buttermilk, oil, and egg. Whisk to combine then add to dry ingredients. Stir until well mixed. Stir in onion and chives.

4. When the oil is at 350°F, drop batter by a heaping teaspoonful into the hot oil. I use my smallest cookie scoop, which measures about .35 ounces, and I fry 6 hushpuppies at a time. Make sure the oil stays at 350°F, and use a large slotted spoon

or wire skimmer to flip the hush-puppies over occasionally so that both sides cook. Fry the hushpuppies for about 4 minutes each then scoop them out using the slotted spoon, and place them on a paper towel-lined baking sheet. Continue frying batches of hushpuppies until all the batter is gone.

5. Serve hot with honey butter or jam if you wish.

Mom's Sweet Corn Chowder

This recipe is based on my mom's corn chowder recipe, which I remember as a dinnertime staple during my childhood. We ate it a lot, and I've always loved it. You can make it any time of year with frozen or even canned corn, but it really shines in the summer with fresh sweet corn cut right off the cob. It is creamy, comforting, and full of flavor—what more can you ask for in a soup?

Serves 6 to 8

8 slices bacon, chopped

2 tablespoons butter

1 cup chopped onion
(about $1/2$ a large onion)

1 pound Yukon gold potatoes, chopped into bite-size pieces (about 3 cups)

4 cups low-sodium chicken broth

3 tablespoons all-purpose flour

2 cups half-and-half

3 cups corn kernels

Salt and pepper

Fresh chives for sprinkling on top

1. In a large soup pot or heavy-bottom Dutch oven, cook bacon over medium heat until bacon is cooked through and crispy. Scoop the bacon out and set it on a plate lined with paper towels. If there is a ton of bacon grease, pour off all but about 1 tablespoon.

2. Add the butter and allow it to melt then add onion and potatoes. Cook, stirring often to keep the potatoes from sticking, until onion is tender, about 5 minutes. Add chicken broth and bring to a simmer. Cover and simmer until potatoes are tender, 15–20 minutes.

3. Combine flour and half-and-half in a glass measuring cup, and whisk

until smooth. Add the half-and-half mixture and the corn to the pot and continue cooking until the soup is slightly thickened and the corn is cooked through, about 5 minutes. Stir in the reserved bacon pieces. Salt and pepper to taste. Serve hot with fresh chives sprinkled on top.

Height of Summer Salad with Green Goddess Dressing

Green goddess dressing is one of my favorite salad dressings. It's full of fresh herb flavor, with a vibrant green color to match. It's at its best during the summer months when herb gardens are overflowing. And wouldn't you know it, salads are at their best during the summer too! Pile your salad bowl high with whatever delicious things happen to be ripe in your garden or whatever catches your eye at the farmer's market. **Dressing makes 1 pint**

For the green goddess dressing

- 1/2 cup buttermilk
- 1/2 cup mayonnaise
- 1/2 cup coarsely chopped fresh parsley leaves
- 1/3 cup sour cream
- 1/4 cup snipped fresh chives
- 2 tablespoons coarsely chopped fresh tarragon
- 1 tablespoon fresh lemon juice
- 1 teaspoon minced or grated fresh garlic
- 1/2 teaspoon salt
- Freshly ground black pepper

For the salad

- Mixed greens or lettuces
- Heirloom cherry tomatoes
- Hard-boiled eggs
- Quick-pickled onions (see Notes for the recipe)
- Carrots
- Scallions
- Celery
- Grilled corn, cut off the cob
- Crumbled bacon
- Cheese of choice
- Avocado
- Cucumbers
- Roasted beets
- Radishes
- Peppers
- Chopped nuts
- Croutons

continued

1. To make the dressing, combine all dressing ingredients in a blender or in the bowl of a food processor, and blend until smooth and a lovely shade of green. Cover and chill until needed.

2. To assemble the salad, start with a bed of lettuces or greens, and add toppings and other components to your liking. Drizzle with dressing and serve.

Notes & Variations

1. Quick-pickled onions are so delicious. Once you've mastered them, you'll find a million excuses to make them. In a small saucepan, combine 1 medium red onion, very thinly sliced, with $1/2$ cup water, $1/4$ cup white vinegar, $1/4$ cup apple cider vinegar, a big pinch of kosher salt, and 1 teaspoon sugar. Simmer on the stove top until the mixture is bright pink and the onions are as tender as you want them. I'm fine with mine tender or a little crunchy. Let cool and eat!

2. Top your salad with grilled chicken or salmon to make it a perfect summer entrée.

Santa Maria Grilled Tri-Tip

Tri-tip is the star of Santa Maria barbecue, a delicious but little-known style of barbecue native to the farms and ranches of the central California coast, where my husband grew up. It's one of the first things he cooked for me when we were dating, and is at least partly responsible for my parents liking him so much. This is one of our go-to dinners, especially when we invite family and friends over on the weekends. It is probably our most requested dish, and I can't take any credit for it! To be super authentic, you would have to cook the meat over red oak on a Santa Maria-style rotisserie, but low and slow on a regular old gas grill has always worked for us. **Serves 8 to 10**

2 1/2 to 3 pounds beef tri-tip

Lemon pepper

Montreal Steak Seasoning

Lawry's Seasoned Salt

1. Lay the tri-tip on a baking sheet and season both sides liberally with lemon pepper, Montreal Steak Seasoning, and Lawry's Seasoned Salt. Cover with plastic wrap and let set at room temperature for 30 minutes.

2. Preheat a gas grill. Place tri-tip on grill over a low flame with the cover down for 15 minutes, then flip, cover, and continue cooking to the desired level of doneness. Ours is usually another 15 minutes for medium. You can use a meat thermometer to check the internal temperature; 145°F for medium-rare, 155°F for medium, and 165°F for medium-well.

continued

3. Remove the tri-tip from the grill, place on a clean cutting board, and cover with aluminum foil. Allow to rest for 15 minutes.

4. Slice into $1/8$-inch-thick slices and serve.

Notes & Variations

1. It occurred to me last year that my husband was spending hours of his life every year slicing tri-tip, and that an electric knife would save him time and allow him to cut thinner slices. Santa brought him an electric knife for Christmas and his tri-tip game has been better than ever!

2. Leftovers can be stored in an airtight container in the fridge. My dad's all-time favorite way to eat grilled tri-tip is straight out of the fridge the next day, and I have to admit, it is delicious cold.

3. Occasionally, we like to make tri-tip sandwiches. We usually just pile thinly sliced tri-tip on crusty rolls and top it with salsa, but you could get fancier with toppings if you wanted to.

4. Sirloin is a great alternative to tri-tip. Season the meat in exactly the same way and follow the same cooking directions, adding enough extra time for the rounder cut of beef to cook to the desired internal temperature. In my opinion, sirloin has a beefier flavor than tri-tip and is a little more tender, which makes it great for sandwiches.

Seafood Boil with New Potatoes, Kielbasa & Corn

My husband requests a seafood boil for dinner on his birthday every year, and it's always a big hit with a crowd. It looks both impressive and festive, and it's quite easy to throw together. You can even scale it up or down based on how many people you're feeding. Depending on what part of the country (or world) you live in, you'll have access to different fresh seafood; use whatever you can find that you like. **Serves 6**

18 to 24 whole baby red potatoes

1 box seafood or shrimp boil seasoning

1 large onion, quartered

2 lemons, quartered

Water

12 ounces smoked sausage or kielbasa, cut into 6 pieces

12 crab legs

3 pounds raw shrimp, peeled and deveined, with tails intact

3 ears fresh corn on the cob, halved

Cajun seasoning, Old Bay seasoning, melted butter, and lemon wedges for serving

1. Put potatoes in a large pot. If you have a pasta pot or a strainer basket (where the pot with holes nestles inside a slightly larger pot), use it! Add seasoning, onion, and lemons to the pot, and fill with water. You don't want to fill your pot to the top with water because you'll be adding lots more stuff to it, but you need to add more than you would if you were just cooking the potatoes. Bring to a boil.

2. Add sausage, wait 5 minutes, then add crab legs and allow to boil for 3-4 more minutes. Add shrimp and corn and cook until shrimp is pink, 4-5 minutes more. Drain off water, replace lid, and let set for 10 minutes, covered.

3. Sprinkle with Cajun seasoning and pour onto a table covered with freezer paper or onto big serving platters. Serve with Old Bay seasoning, more Cajun seasoning, melted butter, and lemon wedges.

Southern Green Beans with Bacon & Onion

My mom has always made green beans with bacon and onion, and it's one of my favorite ways to eat this dinnertime staple. A few summers ago, my husband and I had probably the most delicious green beans I've ever tasted at a Southern restaurant in Minneapolis called Revival. I could taste the bacon and onion, and another ingredient that added an extra layer of complex flavor: red wine vinegar. I came home from that trip and recreated Revival's green beans as best I could remember. We've been eating them this way ever since, especially on summer evenings when the trellis is heavy with long, green beans. **Serves 4 to 6**

1 pound fresh green beans, ends snapped off and broken into 2-inch pieces (3 1/2 to 4 cups)

1/4 cup finely minced fresh onion

4 slices bacon

2 tablespoons butter

2 teaspoons red wine vinegar

Salt

Freshly ground black pepper

1. Place green beans and onion in a medium saucepan. Add enough water to just cover the beans. Place bacon strips on top. Cover and bring to a simmer over medium heat. Cook, covered, until green beans are tender, about 10 minutes.

2. Drain beans and discard bacon. Add butter and vinegar. Salt and pepper to taste. Serve immediately.

Fresh Peaches & Cream Pie

The first time I ever had this pie, my friend Annie brought it to a summer pie contest at church, and it won the top prize quite handily. Annie's pie has such humble ingredients (and not many of them) that you might wonder how it can be so darn good. And I have two answers: magic and fresh peaches. The key is to use the freshest, sweetest, juiciest peaches you can find. The buttery, crunchy graham cracker crust and the sweet, creamy topping are just delicious extras; the peaches are the real stars of the show. **Makes 6 to 8 servings**

For the crust

10 sheets graham crackers

5 tablespoons butter, melted

3 tablespoons granulated sugar

For the pie

6 to 8 peaches, pitted and thinly sliced

1 (14-ounce) can sweetened condensed milk

1/4 cup fresh lemon juice

1. Preheat oven to 350°F.

2. In the bowl of a food processor, pulse or process graham crackers until you get fine crumbs (about 30 seconds). Add butter and sugar and pulse until combined. Press mixture firmly in the bottom and up the sides of a 9-inch pie plate. Bake for 7–10 minutes until golden and set. Set aside and allow to cool completely.

3. When cooled, fill crust as high as you can with peach slices. In a medium bowl, whisk condensed milk and lemon juice until smooth. Pour over peach slices and, using a spatula, spread toward the edges. Serve immediately.

Note

Sometimes I dress up the top of the pie with additional graham cracker crumbs. I just crumble up a couple of crackers and sprinkle on top.

Campfire S'mores Brownies

Over a decade ago, when my blog, Lulu the Baker, was just a few months old, I got the idea to make a batch of brownies that tasted like s'mores. I put a buttery graham cracker crust on the bottom, a layer of fudgy, homemade brownies in the middle, and real marshmallows and chocolate candy bars on top. And wouldn't you know, they were amazing! They really did taste like a brownie/s'mores mash-up. These brownies are one of my favorite recipes I've ever created—the perfect summer dessert, evocative of long, balmy nights and backyard bonfires.

Serves 16 to 20

For the graham cracker layer

> 16 sheets graham crackers
>
> 1/2 cup butter, melted
>
> 1/4 cup granulated sugar

For the brownie layer

> 2 cups granulated sugar
>
> 1 cup butter, softened
>
> 4 eggs
>
> 2 teaspoons vanilla extract
>
> 1 1/2 cups all-purpose flour
>
> 1/3 cup cocoa powder
>
> 1/4 teaspoon salt

For the topping

> 3 cups mini marshmallows
>
> 6 (1.5-ounce) Hershey bars or 9 ounces milk chocolate chips

continued

1. Preheat oven to 350°F. Lightly spray the sides of a 9 x 13-inch baking pan with nonstick cooking spray and set aside.

2. In the bowl of a food processor, pulse or process graham crackers until you get fine crumbs (about 30 seconds) to make the graham cracker layer. Add butter and sugar and pulse until evenly combined. Spread the graham cracker crumb mixture evenly over the bottom of the pan and press firmly.

3. To make the brownie layer, combine sugar and butter in a large bowl or in the bowl of a stand mixer; beat until smooth. Add eggs and vanilla, and beat until incorporated. Add flour, cocoa powder, and salt and beat until just combined. Spread the brownie batter over the graham cracker crust. Bake for 25–30 minutes until the center is set and no longer wet-looking. A toothpick inserted in the center should come out with plenty of crumbs stuck to it, but it shouldn't be covered in wet brownie batter.

4. Sprinkle marshmallows evenly over the top and bake 3–5 more minutes, until marshmallows are puffy and just beginning to turn golden.

5. Remove from the oven and place the chocolate bars evenly on top of the marshmallows. If you're using chocolate chips instead, sprinkle them evenly over the top. They should melt on their own in a minute or so, or you can pop the pan back in the oven for 1 minute. Use a frosting spreader or spatula to spread the melted chocolate evenly over the top. Allow to cool completely before eating!

Note

This makes a lot of brownies, which I think is wonderful! But if you really, really, really want to make fewer brownies, you have my blessing to make half the recipe in an 8-inch square pan and bake it for the same amount of time.

Homemade Vanilla Ice Cream with Hot Fudge Sauce

Homemade ice cream on a hot summer day is hard to beat. A little work and patience turn simple ingredients into a luxurious treat that tastes much better than its store-bought counterpart. And the anticipation is really half the fun. Homemade ice cream is definitely not an instant gratification type of dessert, but that just adds to the excitement of it all: combining sugar and milk and cream, listening to the whir of the ice cream machine and the crunch of the rock salt and ice, and waiting, waiting, waiting for that sweet reward.

Makes about 2 quarts

For the ice cream

2 cups heavy cream

1 cup whole milk

1 (14-ounce) can sweetened condensed milk

2 teaspoons vanilla extract

A pinch of salt

For the hot fudge sauce

1 1/2 cups granulated sugar

1/2 cup water

1/4 cup corn syrup

4 tablespoons butter

3 ounces 60% or semi-sweet chocolate

1 ounce milk chocolate

A generous pinch of salt

1 teaspoon vanilla extract

continued

1. To make the ice cream, combine all ice cream ingredients in a medium bowl and whisk until combined.

2. Pour the mixture into the bowl of an ice cream freezer and freeze according to the manufacturer's instructions. When the ice cream is frozen (it takes about an hour in our machine), scoop ice cream into a container with a tight-fitting lid, and place in the freezer until firm and scoopable, at least 4 hours.

3. While the ice cream is hardening in the freezer, make the hot fudge sauce. Combine all hot fudge ingredients except the vanilla in a medium saucepan over medium heat. Stir occasionally and bring to a boil then boil for 7 minutes. Remove from heat and stir in the vanilla. Pour the hot fudge sauce into a blender, put the lid on slightly askew, and hold it in place with a kitchen towel to let steam escape while not burning yourself. Blend the hot fudge sauce for 4 minutes until it is satiny.

4. When the ice cream is hard enough to scoop, serve it up topped with hot fudge sauce.

Notes & Variations

1. You can make lots of different fruity ice cream flavors by stirring $1/2$ cup of fruit purée into the mixture before churning it. Try strawberry, raspberry, blackberry, peach, or a mix!

2. If you just can't wait for the ice cream to harden, you can eat it as soon as it's done churning. It'll be the texture of soft serve.

3. You can store leftover fudge sauce in the fridge in a container with a tight-fitting lid. The sugar will recrystallize, so just reheat it before serving. 1 minute 30 seconds in the microwave works well, stirring every 30 seconds.

Sugar-Topped Shortcake Biscuits

Can you even think of a more quintessential summer dessert than strawberry shortcake? The juicy, ruby-red berries that smell like candy, the piles of sweet whipped cream, lighter than air, and the cakey, vanilla-scented base. I love strawberry shortcake in all of its many incarnations. It is delicious with angel food cake, yellow cake, and pound cake. But my very favorite treat upon which to build strawberry shortcake is a slightly sweet, crumbly, buttery biscuit. They're so easy to make, and the textures and flavors add just the loveliest contrast to the berries and whipped cream. Feel free to swap out strawberries for whatever kind of fruit you fancy. You really can't go wrong! **Makes 6 to 8 biscuits**

2 cups all-purpose flour

3 tablespoons granulated sugar

1 tablespoon baking powder

1/2 teaspoon salt

6 tablespoons cold butter, cut into chunks

3/4 cup milk plus more for brushing on top of the biscuits

2 teaspoons coarse sugar

1. Preheat the oven to 425°F. Line a baking sheet with a piece of parchment paper or a silicone baking mat.

2. In the bowl of a food processor, combine flour, granulated sugar, baking powder, and salt; process for a few seconds just to combine. Add cold butter chunks and pulse about 10 times until the butter starts to be incorporated into the dry ingredients. Add 3/4 cup milk and continue pulsing the mixture until the dough begins to stick together in clumps.

3. Turn the dough out onto a floured counter, and shape it into a

rectangle about 1 inch thick. Cut the dough into 6 or 8 equal squares. Place the biscuits on the baking sheet. Brush the tops with the remaining milk, and sprinkle with coarse sugar.

4. Bake for 15 minutes until the edges are golden brown. Remove from the oven and allow to cool. Serve warm or at room temperature, topped with sweetened fruit and fresh whipped cream.

Summer Fruit Cobbler

To me, warm desserts filled with sweet fruit are just about perfection. This is my favorite cobbler recipe in the whole world for lots of reasons: it is ridiculously easy to make; you can use all different kinds of fruit and get amazing results; and most importantly, it tastes heavenly. **Serves 8 to 12**

8 cups fresh fruit (blackberries, raspberries, blueberries, cherries (halved and pitted), diced peaches, diced rhubarb, chopped strawberries, etc.)

2 tablespoons fresh lemon juice

2 cups granulated sugar

2 cups all-purpose flour

2 eggs

12 tablespoons (1 1/2 sticks) butter, melted

Sweetened whipped cream or ice cream for serving

1. Preheat oven to 375°F. Lightly spray a 9 x 13-inch baking pan with non-stick cooking spray.

2. Spread fruit evenly in pan and sprinkle with lemon juice.

3. In a medium bowl, combine sugar, flour, and egg until crumbly. Spread mixture evenly over the top of the berries. Drizzle melted butter evenly over the top of the crumble mixture.

4. Bake for 40–45 minutes, until the topping is golden and bubbly. Serve warm with sweetened whipped cream or ice cream.

Notes

1. You can use any mix of fruit you like. We've made this dozens of times over the years and with dozens of different combinations,

and every single one of them has been delicious.

2. You can easily cut the recipe in half and bake it in an 8-inch square baking dish for the same amount of time.

3. In the winter and early spring, we use frozen fruit instead of fresh fruit, and it turns out exactly the same. Just increase the baking time until the top is golden.

autumn

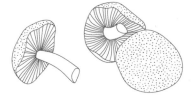

AUTUMN AT THE FARMHOUSE is a feast for the senses. The days get shorter and shorter, going from warm and balmy to crisp and blustery. The pumpkins we planted in the garden months ago are finally the fat, orange orbs they promised to be. Apples and pears go straight from the tree to the kitchen, destined to become sauce and leather and pie filling. We find ways to save summer's garden bounty: tomatoes and peppers become jars of salsa, the last of the berries and corn get frozen so they can bring us a taste of summer all winter long. We dust off the press and invite friends over to make apple cider and eat donuts and chili in the yard. The leaves on the trees turn fiery shades of red and orange before falling to the ground, where they get raked into piles that provide hours of jumping fun. For me, autumn at the farmhouse is a season of magic and wonder.

Farmhouse Weekends in Autumn

go leaf peeping • pick apples from an orchard • visit a pumpkin patch

• wander through a corn maze • sip freshly pressed apple cider

• harvest cranberries in a cranberry marsh

• forage for wild mushrooms (with a knowledgeable guide!)

• harvest wine grapes • go crabbing • eat hot donuts covered in sugar

Apple Dutch Baby

Dutch babies are a fun breakfast treat. This one, filled with tart apples and a gooey cinnamon-sugar sauce, is even more delicious and impressive, filling the whole house with the tempting aromas of cinnamon and apples as it bakes. It's easy to make and cooks fairly quickly, so you don't even have to wake up early on weekend mornings to make this cozy brunch dish for your family and friends.

Serves 6 to 8

For the apple layer

1/2 cup butter

1/2 cup brown sugar

1/3 cup granulated sugar

2 teaspoons cinnamon

1 pound apples, peeled, cored, and thinly sliced (about 2 large apples)

For the batter

1 cup all-purpose flour

2 tablespoons granulated sugar

1/2 teaspoon salt

4 eggs, beaten

1 cup whole milk

1 tablespoon vanilla extract

Powdered sugar and maple syrup for serving, optional

1. Preheat oven to 400°F. Add the butter to a 12-inch cast iron skillet and put it in the oven.

2. While the butter melts, combine brown sugar, granulated sugar, and cinnamon in a small bowl. When the butter has melted, remove the skillet from the oven and set it on a heat-proof surface like your stove top. Add the sugar mixture to the skillet and whisk to combine. Add the sliced apples and toss gently until the apples are coated with the sugar mixture. Return the skillet to the oven and cook for 10 minutes, until the mixture is bubbly.

3. While the apples cook, prepare the batter. Combine flour, sugar, and salt in a large bowl. Add eggs, milk, and vanilla. Whisk until smooth.

4. When the apples have cooked for 10 minutes, pour the batter as evenly as you can over the top of the apples, and bake for an additional 20 minutes. The batter will spread out and puff up on the sides.

5. The Dutch baby is done when it is quite tall and brown on the sides, and when a knife inserted in the center comes out wet, but clear. Cut into wedges and serve with powdered sugar for sprinkling or maple syrup for drizzling.

Note

A 12-inch skillet has almost the same volume as a 9 x 13-inch pan. If you have a 12-inch skillet, you should absolutely use it for this recipe, but if you don't, the 9 x 13-inch pan is a fine substitute.

Caramel Sticky Buns

A caramel sticky bun is a cinnamon roll's sassy cousin. Instead of cream cheese frosting or a vanilla glaze, caramel sticky buns are topped (or bottomed, depending on what point in the baking process you're talking about) with a luscious butterscotch sauce that gets stickier and more candy-like as it cools. It sticks in your teeth in the very best of ways, and leaves you fingers syrupy with butter and brown sugar. These are an impressive weekend treat, sure to delight anyone lucky enough to get one. **Makes 12 sticky buns**

For the dough

- $1/4$ cup warm water
- 1 tablespoon active dry yeast
- 1 cup warm milk (microwaved for about 1 minute)
- $1/3$ cup granulated sugar
- $1/3$ cup butter, melted (microwaved for about 1 minute)
- 1 teaspoon salt
- 1 egg
- 4 cups all-purpose flour

For the sticky topping

- $1 1/2$ cups butter, softened
- $3/4$ cup brown sugar

For the filling

- $1/4$ cup butter, softened
- $3/4$ cup granulated sugar
- 1 tablespoon cinnamon

continued

1. To make the dough, combine the warm water and yeast in a small bowl or glass measuring cup. Set aside in a warm spot for 10 minutes until the yeast is activated and the mixture begins to grow in volume. Meanwhile, combine the warm milk, sugar, melted butter, salt, and egg in a large bowl or in the bowl of a stand mixer. Add the proofed yeast mixture and mix to combine. Add the flour. If you are using a stand mixer, switch to the dough hook attachment at this point. If you are making the bread dough in a large bowl, stir it with a wooden spoon until it gets too difficult then use your hands. Either way, knead the dough for 5 minutes until smooth and elastic. At this point, the dough might still be slightly sticky, and that's OK. Place the dough in a bowl that's been sprayed with non-stick baking spray or lightly coated with oil, cover it with a damp towel, and set in a warm place to rise until doubled in volume, about 1 hour.

2. While the dough is rising, prepare the topping. Beat the butter and brown sugar for the topping in a medium bowl until fluffy. Grease a 9 x 13-inch cake pan. Spread the topping as evenly as you can in the bottom of the pan; set aside.

3. When the dough has doubled in volume, remove the towel, punch down the dough, and knead it lightly on a well-floured surface. Roll it into a large rectangle that measures at least 12 inches on the short side. Spread the softened butter for the filling evenly over the entire surface of the dough rectangle, keeping one of the shorter edges butter-free. Combine the sugar and cinnamon for the filling in a small bowl then spread the cinnamon sugar over the butter on the dough. Spread the cinnamon sugar all the way to the edges (except the edge you are leaving alone).

4. Roll the rectangle into a long cylinder. Start at the short end of the rectangle opposite from the butterless end, rolling tightly but not too tightly. Use a sharp knife to cut the cylinder into 12 equal slices. Evenly space slices in the prepared pan. Cover with plastic wrap, and set in a warm place to rise for 30 minutes.

5. Preheat oven to 350°F. When the sticky buns have risen noticeably, remove the plastic wrap, place the pan on a large rimmed baking sheet, and place it in the oven. Bake for 30 minutes until the sticky topping is bubbling and the tops of the buns are deeply golden. If the tops of the buns are getting too brown before the time is up, loosely lay a piece of aluminum foil across the top for the remainder of the baking time. Remove the sticky buns from the oven and allow to cool for exactly 5 minutes.

6. Wearing oven mitts or using hot pads, place a large, rimmed baking sheet or a large serving platter over the pan of sticky buns. Hold one hand under the pan and the other hand on top of the baking sheet or serving platter to hold them tightly together then flip the whole thing over. Immediately set the pan or serving platter down on the counter (without spilling any of the hot caramel topping), and remove the pan. If any topping is still in the bottom of the baking pan, scoop it out with a rubber spatula and put it on top of the sticky buns. Serve warm.

Variations

You can use $1\frac{1}{2}$ cups chopped nuts in the topping if you want! We like both pecans and hazelnuts.

Gingery Pumpkin Muffins

I love all kinds of pumpkin muffins—the sugary sweet, cakey ones, the ones full of chocolate chips, the ones with spicy crumbles on top, the ones with a swirl of cream cheese mixed in—but these just might be my favorite. They are unfussy, with no unnecessary extras thrown in, and just a sprinkling of oats on top. They are light in texture and big on flavor, with lots of ginger and cinnamon, and just a hint of nutmeg. They are simple and wholesome and delicious. This recipe is adapted from one I had at an event catered by Clyde Common, a wonderful restaurant in Portland, Oregon. **Makes 12 muffins**

$1/3$ cup butter, softened

$1/3$ cup granulated sugar

$1/3$ cup brown sugar

1 egg

1 egg yolk

$2/3$ cup canned pumpkin purée

$1/3$ cup sour cream

1 teaspoon vanilla extract

$1\,1/3$ cups all-purpose flour

$1/2$ teaspoon baking soda

$1/2$ teaspoon baking powder

$5/8$ teaspoon salt ($1/2$ teaspoon plus $1/8$ teaspoon)

$5/8$ teaspoon ground ginger ($1/2$ teaspoon plus $1/8$ teaspoon)

$5/8$ teaspoon ground cinnamon ($1/2$ teaspoon plus $1/8$ teaspoon)

$1/8$ teaspoon ground nutmeg

2 to 3 tablespoons quick cooking oats for sprinkling on top

continued

1. Preheat oven to 350°F and spray 12 muffin cups with nonstick baking spray, or line them with paper liners.

2. In a large bowl or in the bowl of a stand mixer, beat butter, granulated sugar, and brown sugar on medium speed until creamy, about 1 minute. Add egg and egg yolk and beat until smooth, scraping down the sides and bottom of the bowl with a rubber spatula as needed. Add pumpkin purée, sour cream, and vanilla and beat until smooth.

3. In a medium bowl, combine flour, baking soda, baking powder, salt, and spices. Add the dry ingredients to the mixer and beat on low just until combined. Use a rubber spatula to scrape down the sides of the bowl and make sure everything is mixed in, but be careful not to overmix.

4. Divide the mixture evenly among the 12 muffin cups. Sprinkle a pinch of oats on each muffin.

5. Bake for 19–21 minutes, until the muffins are puffed and set, and a toothpick inserted in the center of a muffin comes out clean.

6. Allow to cool slightly before serving.

Note

Even though these muffins are excellent on their own and don't need any adornments, they do taste really good with a swipe of cinnamon-honey butter on them. Combine equal parts room temperature butter and honey, and stir in cinnamon to taste.

Sweet Potato & Sausage Breakfast Hash

If you're in need of a hearty fall breakfast, look no further! This sweet and savory twist on classic breakfast hash is full of autumnal flavors and beautiful colors: the orange mellowness of sweet potatoes; the herb-filled deliciousness of sausage; the mild freshness of emerald green spinach; the earthiness of mushrooms. Topped with fried eggs and garnished with fresh thyme, it's a warm and comforting breakfast feast that will send you on your weekend adventures with full and happy bellies. **Serves 4 to 6**

1 pound raw orange sweet potatoes or yams, peeled and cut into 1/2-inch cubes

Olive oil

Salt and freshly ground pepper

1 pound bulk breakfast sausage

1 medium yellow onion, diced

4 ounces white button mushrooms, cleaned and chopped (about 3 cups)

2 cloves garlic, minced

2 to 3 ounces fresh spinach, chopped (4 to 6 cups loosely packed spinach leaves)

1 tablespoon fresh thyme leaves, coarsely chopped, plus extra whole leaves for garnish

4 to 6 eggs

1. Preheat oven to 425°F. You can do this before you peel and cube the sweet potatoes if you want to use every minute of your morning wisely. Spread the sweet potato cubes in a single layer on a rimmed baking sheet. Drizzle with about 1 tablespoon olive oil, sprinkle with salt and pepper, and toss until all the cubes are coated. Roast the sweet potatoes for 20–25 minutes, tossing every 10 minutes or so to keep them from burning or sticking.

2. While the sweet potatoes roast, put a large skillet over medium heat. Crumble the breakfast sausage into the pan, and cook until browned and cooked through, about 10

continued

minutes. Remove the sausage to a paper towel-lined plate.

3. If the skillet looks dry, add a drizzle of olive oil. Add onion and mushrooms, and sauté over medium heat 5-7 minutes. Add garlic and sauté 2 minutes more. Add cooked sausage, chopped spinach, and thyme. Cook about 5 minutes more.

4. As soon as the sweet potatoes are crispy on the outside and tender on the inside, add them to the skillet. Toss everything together gently, and salt and pepper to taste.

5. Make 4-6 small wells in the breakfast hash (depending on how many people you are feeding), and crack an egg into each well. Sprinkle just the eggs lightly with salt and pepper, cover, and cook until the eggs are cooked to your liking. Garnish with more fresh thyme leaves, and serve immediately.

Variations

Feel free to get creative with the ingredients of this breakfast hash. If you picked up some fancy mushrooms at the farmers market, for example, or you have other greens in your garden besides spinach, you have my permission to mix it up!

Harvest Spice Fruit & Nut Granola

It's no secret that I love granola, especially homemade granola. To me, it tastes worlds better than any kind you can get at the store, and you can customize it to your liking. This recipe is perfect for autumn. It has oats and nuts and seeds, sweet maple and brown sugar flavors, and warm spices paired with autumnal dried fruits. As it bakes, it makes the whole house smell like a big, cozy bowl of fall-flavored oatmeal. **Makes 4 1/2 to 5 cups granola**

1 1/2 cups old-fashioned rolled oats

1/2 cup raw, shelled
pumpkin seeds (pepitas)

1/2 cup raw, shelled sunflower seeds

1/2 cup finely chopped pecans

1/4 cup brown sugar

1/4 cup pure maple syrup

1/4 cup extra virgin olive oil

1/2 teaspoon salt

1/2 teaspoon pumpkin pie spice

1/2 cup finely chopped dried apples

1/2 cup golden raisins

1/2 cup sweetened dried cranberries

1. Preheat oven to 300°F. Line 2 large, rimmed baking sheets with parchment paper or silicone baking mats. Set 1 aside.

2. In a large bowl, combine oats, pumpkin and sunflower seeds, pecans, and brown sugar. Toss to combine.

3. In a medium, microwave-safe bowl or large glass measuring cup, combine maple syrup, olive oil, salt, and pumpkin pie spice. Microwave for 30 seconds then whisk until combined. Pour the liquid over the oat mixture and toss until evenly coated.

4. Pour the oat mixture onto 1 of the prepared baking sheets and spread it into an even layer. Bake for 45 minutes, stirring every 15 minutes.

5. As soon as you get the granola out of the oven, use a spatula to scrape it onto the unused baking sheet. Spread it into an even layer, add the dried fruits, and allow it to cool completely. When the granola is cool, use your hands to break it into small pieces.

Variations

Granola is so easy to customize. Keep the main elements of the recipe (like the amounts of things) the same, but change up the type of nuts and seeds, the sweeteners, the spices, and the dried fruits to your liking.

Autumn Broccoli Salad

Full disclosure: I could eat this broccoli salad all year long, not just in the fall. But it is really, really good in the cool weather of autumn when you can get fresh, local broccoli and juicy apples straight from the orchard. One of my favorite things about this salad is the poppy seed vinaigrette. Store bought poppy seed dressing has a tendency to be thick, gloppy, and overly sweet, but this vinaigrette version is tantalizingly tangy, and doesn't overshadow all of the other flavorful salad components. **Serves 12**

For the poppy seed vinaigrette

- 3/4 cup granulated sugar
- 3/4 cup white vinegar
- Dash of red wine vinegar
- 1/2 cup vegetable or canola oil
- 1/4 cup Dijon mustard
- 1 tablespoon poppy seeds
- 1/2 teaspoon salt

For the salad

- 24 ounces fresh broccoli florets, chopped into bite-size pieces (about 7 1/2 cups)
- 1 cup dried, sweetened cranberries
- 1/2 cup cashews, chopped
- 1/2 cup shelled roasted, salted sunflower seeds
- 1 apple, diced
- 1/2 red onion, diced
- 1 pound bacon, cooked and crumbled

1. To make the dressing, combine all ingredients in a container with a tight-fitting lid. Shake until completely combined. Refrigerate until needed.

2. To make the salad, combine all ingredients in a large bowl. Toss with dressing to taste, and serve.

Cast Iron Skillet Sweet Cornbread

I've always loved cornbread, but when my husband introduced me to his secret family recipe, I became a true fanatic. I tinkered with the original Bahen family recipe a little bit to make it truly from scratch (no premade mixes of any kind here!), and we're baking it in a buttery, preheated cast iron skillet for a deliciously golden crust on the bottom (and oodles of ambiance). Best served with copious amounts of honey butter. **Makes 8 servings**

1/4 cup butter

1 1/4 cups all-purpose flour

1/2 cup granulated sugar

1/4 cup cornmeal

1 1/2 teaspoons baking powder

1/2 teaspoon baking soda

1/2 teaspoon salt

3/4 cup buttermilk

1/4 cup vegetable or canola oil

1 whole egg plus 1 egg yolk

1. Preheat oven to 350°F. Add the butter to a 9-inch cast iron skillet and put it in the oven while it preheats.

2. Combine flour, sugar, cornmeal, baking powder, baking soda, and salt in a large bowl and whisk until blended.

3. In a glass measuring cup, combine buttermilk, oil, and eggs, and stir gently until combined. Pour the wet ingredients into the dry ingredients and whisk until just combined. It's ok if there are still lumps.

4. When the butter in the skillet has melted, pour the melted butter into the batter, and whisk until smooth. Pour the batter back into the hot skillet, and bake until golden on top and completely baked through,

20–25 minutes. Serve warm with honey butter.

Notes & Variations

1. You can use this exact same recipe to make 12 regular-size muffins. Line 12 muffin cups with paper liners or spray with nonstick baking spray. Melt the butter in a small saucepan over low heat, or in a heat-proof bowl in the microwave. Bake the muffins for 15–18 minutes.

2. You can also double the recipe and bake it in a greased 9 x 13-inch baking dish. Use 3 whole eggs total, and increase the baking time to 35 minutes.

Classic Beef & Bean Chili

Chili is my go-to fall dinner. Apple picking? Chili for dinner! Pumpkin patching? Chili for dinner! Raking leaves on a cloudy, blustery afternoon? Chili, most definitely, for dinner! When my husband and I were newlyweds, I started trying different chili recipes, hoping to find a favorite. It took me years to find this one. It was shared by my Aunt Gigi in a family reunion cookbook, and after one bite, I knew I'd found the last chili recipe I'd ever need. It's rich and savory and hearty— the perfect dinner for any crisp evening. We serve ours topped with sour cream, grated cheddar cheese, and crumbled Fritos. **Makes 8 to 10 servings**

2 pounds ground beef

1 (29-ounce) can diced tomatoes, undrained

Water

1 (29-ounce) can tomato sauce

1 (29-ounce) can kidney beans, undrained

1 (29-ounce) can pinto beans, undrained

1 cup diced onion

1 (4-ounce) can diced green chiles

1/4 cup diced celery

2 teaspoons cumin

2 tablespoons chili powder

2 teaspoons salt

Freshly ground black pepper

1. In the bottom of a large Dutch oven, brown the ground beef, and drain off the grease.

2. Drain the diced tomatoes into a 2-cup liquid measuring cup. If necessary, add enough water to make 2 cups of liquid. Add the tomatoes and liquid to the Dutch oven.

3. Add all remaining ingredients. Bring to a boil, cover, and reduce heat. Simmer for 2–3 hours, stirring every 15 minutes. Serve hot, topped with sour cream, grated cheddar cheese, crumbled Fritos, diced onions or green onions, or your favorite chili toppings.

continued

Notes

1. During tomato season, you can use 3 medium tomatoes, chopped, in place of the canned tomatoes. Replace the tomato liquid/water combo with 2 cups water.

2. You can also use fresh green chiles, small diced, in place of the canned chiles. Fun fact: We actually roast all the chiles and peppers we grow that we can't manage to eat fresh, and use them all year instead of canned chiles. It's an easy farmhouse week-end project. Rub clean, dry chiles/peppers with olive oil, place in a single layer on a rimmed baking sheet, and sprinkle with salt and pepper. Place them in the top $1/3$ of the oven with the broiler turned on. Broil just until the skin is blistered and charred (this will take 5 minutes or less) then flip the peppers over with tongs and broil for the same amount of time on the other side. Dump the charred peppers into a paper grocery bag, roll the top down to close the bag completely, and allow the peppers to steam as they cool. Once they're cool, you can peel, seed, and use them right away, or freeze them for later. You don't even have to peel or seed the ones you freeze until after you thaw them. It's so easy, it takes about 10 seconds.

3. Anaheim peppers or canned green chiles make a mild chili. You can use poblano peppers for medium heat, or jalapeños if you like your chili spicy.

Smoky White Bean Chili with Chicken

This recipe is for anyone who says they don't like chili. I love chili, both the classic tomato-based version, and this lighter variation with a Tex-Mex flair. A lot of white bean chili recipes rely on the addition of sour cream or even cream cheese to the broth to give it flavor, but I love this recipe because it has tons of flavor all on its own. It's delicious as is, and the toppings are just the icing on the cake. Make both kinds of chili and invite friends over for dinner on a cool autumn evening. **Serves 8**

2 tablespoons olive oil

1 cup finely chopped onion (about $1/2$ a large onion)

1 small can diced green chiles (or $1/2$ cup diced fresh green chiles)

2 tablespoons minced garlic (about 6 cloves garlic)

4 (15-ounce) cans white beans, drained

6 cups low-sodium chicken broth

2 teaspoons cumin

2 teaspoons dried oregano

1 teaspoon smoked sweet paprika

$1/2$ teaspoon coriander

$1/2$ teaspoon salt

Freshly ground black pepper

1 to $1^1/2$ pounds shredded rotisserie chicken (Smoked chicken or BBQ rotisserie chicken is even better)

1 cup heavy cream

continued

1. Heat olive oil in a large, heavy-bottom pot or Dutch oven over medium heat. Add onion and chiles, and sauté until onion is tender and translucent, about 5 minutes. Add garlic and sauté until garlic is fragrant, 1–2 minutes more.

2. Pour 1 can of beans into a shallow bowl and mash with a fork until smooth. Alternately, you can pulse them in a food processor. Add mashed beans, remaining canned beans, chicken broth, and all spices to the pot and bring to a boil. Reduce heat and simmer, covered, for at least 30 minutes.

3. Add chicken and heavy cream and continue cooking until the chili is heated through. Serve with grated cheese, sour cream, crushed tortilla chips, diced avocado, or chopped cilantro for topping.

Note

See Classic Beef & Bean Chili (page 122) for notes on increasing the heat if you like a spicier chili, and instructions on roasting your own peppers.

Creamy Chicken & Wild Rice Soup

This is one of my favorite soups! I love it all year, but it seems especially appropriate for fall. It is savory and comforting, and warms you up from the inside out on cold nights. This recipe makes a lot, so you can make it once and have leftovers for the next night; it's the gift that keeps on giving. **Serves 8 to 10**

1/4 cup butter

2 cups diced carrots

2 cups diced celery

1 cup diced onion

1/4 cup all-purpose flour

8 cups low-sodium chicken broth

2 pounds chopped, cooked chicken

3 cups cooked wild rice blend (a mix of wild and long grain rice)

1 cup heavy cream

1 teaspoon poultry seasoning

1/2 teaspoon salt

Freshly ground black pepper

1. In a large, heavy-bottom pot or Dutch oven, melt the butter over medium heat. Add carrots, celery, and onion, and sauté until tender, about 10 minutes. Stir in the flour and cook until it has disappeared, about 1 minute. Add chicken broth and stir.

2. Add chicken, rice, cream, and poultry seasoning and continue cooking until everything is heated through, 7–10 minutes more. Salt and pepper to taste, and serve.

Note

I can sometimes find unseasoned, fully-cooked wild rice blends at the grocery store in the microwavable rice section. 2 (8-ounce) packages will give you just about the right amount of rice for this recipe, and will cut down on work and cooking time.

Fall Harvest Salad with Fresh Cranberry Vinaigrette

I love a good green salad no matter what time of year it is, especially when it makes use of the bounty of the season. In the fall, that means orchard fruits like apples and pears, cool weather-loving lettuces, and crunchy nuts. This autumnal salad is colorful and flavorful, with a tart, homemade vinaigrette that is an arresting shade of magenta thanks to fresh cranberries. You can make it all season long, even into the early winter months when fresh cranberries are easy to find. I'm forever indebted to my friend Amy for sharing this recipe with me years ago. **Serves 8 to 10**

For the dressing

1 cup fresh cranberries

1/2 cup granulated sugar

1/2 cup apple cider vinegar

1/4 cup frozen apple juice concentrate, thawed

1 teaspoon salt

1 teaspoon ground mustard powder

1 teaspoon grated onion

1 cup vegetable oil

For the salad

1 (10-ounce) package mixed salad greens

1 small red apple, diced

1 small green or yellow pear, diced

1 cup freshly shredded Parmesan cheese

1/2 cup fresh pomegranate arils

1/4 cup slivered almonds, toasted

1/4 cup chopped pecans, toasted

1. In a food processor or blender, combine all the dressing ingredients except the oil. Process until smooth. With the machine running, add oil in a steady stream until the dressing is bright pink and creamy. Pour the dressing into a pretty, pour-friendly container and refrigerate until ready to serve.

2. To assemble the salad, combine all ingredients in a large bowl. Toss and serve with the dressing on the side.

Note

You can toss roasted winter squash on top of this salad to make it extra hearty!

Black-Bottom Pecan Pie Bars

Pecan pie always makes me think of my father-in-law. I didn't grow up eating pecan pie, although I'm pretty sure both my parents like it. My father-in-law insists on making it every year for Thanksgiving, and it finally occurred to me that if Pop makes it every year, it must be good. And it is! These bars have all the best qualities of classic pecan pie—a butterscotchy, stick-to-your-teeth filling and crunchy, toasty pecans—with a few delicious twists. Instead of a pastry crust, these bars have an easy, press-in shortbread crust with a tasty layer of chocolate on top, and making bars instead of a traditional pie results in a perfect ratio of crust-to-filling. You'll have a hard time eating just one! **Makes 24 or more bars**

For the crust

- 1 2/3 cups all-purpose flour
- 2/3 cup powdered sugar
- 1/4 teaspoon salt
- 2/3 cup butter, softened

For the filling

- 1/2 cup butter
- 1 2/3 cups brown sugar
- 1 cup light corn syrup
- 4 eggs
- 1 tablespoon vanilla extract
- 1/2 teaspoon salt
- 1 scant cup semisweet chocolate chips
- 1 1/3 cups finely chopped pecans

continued

1. Preheat oven to 350°F. Line a 9 x 13-inch baking pan with aluminum foil, and generously spray the foil with nonstick baking spray.

2. To prepare the crust, combine flour, sugar, and salt in a large bowl or in the bowl of a stand mixer. Add softened butter and beat until the mixture is crumbly and the butter is thoroughly distributed. Press the crumb mixture evenly into the bottom of the prepared pan, and bake for 15–20 minutes until the edges just begin to brown.

3. While the crust bakes, prepare the filling. In a large saucepan, melt the butter. Whisk in brown sugar and corn syrup, and stir until brown sugar is dissolved and mixture is hot. Remove from heat and allow to cool until the crust is finished baking. After cool, whisk in eggs, vanilla, and salt, whisking until completely smooth.

4. When the crust is finished prebaking, pull it out of the oven. Scatter the chocolate chips evenly over the bottom of the crust. Top with an even layer of chopped pecans. Carefully pour the filling over the top.

5. Bake for 25 minutes. The filling will initially puff up, but should begin to settle back down when done, and the bars will jiggle as a whole mass when you shake the pan.

6. Remove from the oven and allow to cool completely. Lift the bars out of the baking dish using the foil, fold the foil down, and cut the bars. Serve at room temperature.

Variation

Here's a bit of a wild suggestion, but I promise it's delicious: serve the bars topped with sliced fresh bananas and whipped cream.

Farmstand Apple Cider Donut Holes

Picking apples in the fall is one of my favorite seasonal activities. We have lots of apple trees in our yard now, but before we had our own apples, we loved going to local orchards to stock up on our favorite varieties for pressing cider, making pies, and eating fresh. And the best part of visiting a local orchard is the fresh, hot, homemade apple cider donuts! Since we just pick our own apples now, we have to make our own apple cider donuts. This recipe is a perfect one to make at home. The batter mixes up quickly with easy-to-find ingredients, and you just scoop and drop to make deliciously spiced, apple-flavored donut holes.

Makes about 42 donut holes

Canola or peanut oil (or your favorite type of frying oil)

$2 1/4$ cups all-purpose flour

$1/2$ cup granulated sugar

$1/4$ cup brown sugar

$1 1/2$ teaspoons baking powder

$1/2$ teaspoon baking soda

$1/2$ teaspoon salt

$1/2$ teaspoon cinnamon

$1/2$ teaspoon nutmeg

$1/4$ teaspoon ground cloves

2 eggs

$1/2$ cup unsweetened applesauce

$1/2$ cup sour cream

$1/4$ cup apple juice concentrate, thawed

2 tablespoons butter, melted and cooled

$1/2$ teaspoon vanilla extract

Cinnamon sugar (1 cup sugar plus 1 tablespoon cinnamon)

continued

1. Pour 3 inches of oil into a Dutch oven or heavy-bottom pot. Place over medium heat and bring up to 350°F. Line a rimmed baking sheet with several layers of paper towels and set aside.

2. In a large bowl, combine flour, sugar, brown sugar, baking powder, baking soda, salt, cinnamon, nutmeg, and cloves.

3. In a medium bowl or large glass measuring cup, whisk eggs, applesauce, sour cream, apple juice concentrate, melted butter, and vanilla. Pour this mixture into the dry ingredients and whisk until mostly smooth.

4. When the oil is at the correct temperature, drop the batter by heaping tablespoons into the oil. Fry the donuts for about 3 minutes, flipping them once halfway through. Fry only 5 to 6 donut holes at a time.

5. When the donuts are puffed and deep golden brown, scoop them out using a slotted spoon, and place them on the paper towel–lined baking sheet. Continue frying batches of donuts until all the batter is gone.

6. Toss the warm donuts with cinnamon sugar and serve warm.

Note

You can make this entire recipe with just one person, but it is certainly easier (and more fun!) to have a helper. One person can do the frying and the other person can do the cinnamon sugar.

Old-Fashioned Sugar Donuts

Sugar donuts are my first choice at the donut shop every single time. Who can resist a hot, freshly fried pillow of yeasty dough dredged in granulated sugar? If they're sold out, I'll happily get something else, but my first donut love will always and forever be a sugar donut. And guess what? They're easy to make at home! We've made these old-fashioned treats on Halloween when the kids are done trick-or-treating, and on Fall afternoons when we have friends over to press cider in the front yard. We sometime skip cutting holes out of the middle, but you certainly can if you want to. **Makes about 20 (3-inch) donuts**

1/4 cup warm water

1 tablespoon active dry yeast

1 cup warm milk (microwaved for about 1 minute)

1/3 cup granulated sugar

1/3 cup butter, melted (microwaved for about 1 minute)

1 teaspoon salt

1 egg

A pinch of nutmeg

4 cups all-purpose flour

Canola or peanut oil (or your favorite type of frying oil)

1 cup granulated sugar for coating warm donuts

1. To make the dough, combine the warm water and yeast in a small bowl or glass measuring cup. Set aside in a warm spot for 10 minutes until the yeast is activated and the mixture begins to grow in volume. Meanwhile, combine the warm milk, sugar, melted butter, salt, egg, and nutmeg in a large bowl or in the bowl of a stand mixer. Add the proofed yeast mixture and mix to combine. Add the flour. If you are using a stand mixer, switch to the dough hook attachment at this point. If you are making the bread dough in a large bowl, stir it with a wooden spoon until it gets too difficult then use your hands. Either way,

continued

knead the dough for 5 minutes until smooth and elastic. At this point, the dough might still be slightly sticky, and that's OK. Place the dough in a bowl that's been sprayed with non-stick baking spray or lightly coated with oil, cover it with a damp towel, and set in a warm place to rise until doubled in volume, about 1 hour.

2. When the dough has doubled in volume, turn it out onto a well-floured work surface, and knead it for about 1 minute. Roll it out to a 3/4-inch thickness and use a 2 1/2-inch biscuit cutter to cut rounds. If you want to, you can use a smaller circle to cut out holes, but they're kind of a hassle to fry up, so we sometimes skip that step. Place the donuts about 1 inch apart on a parchment-lined baking sheet sprinkled with flour. Collect and reroll the scraps of dough as many times as needed until all of the dough is cut into circles. Cover the donuts and let rise in a warm place for 30 minutes.

3. While the donuts are rising for the second time, fill a heavy-bottom pot or Dutch oven with at least 2 inches of oil. Place the pot over medium heat and bring the oil up to 365°F.

Line a large, rimmed baking sheet with paper towels.

4. When the donuts are done rising, carefully put 3 donuts at a time into the hot oil. Fry for 1 minute until golden brown on the bottom then flip using a large slotted spoon or wire skimmer. Fry for another minute until the other side is also golden brown then scoop the donuts out and place them on the paper towel–lined baking sheet to cool. Continuing frying donuts in batches of 3 until all of the donuts are cooked.

5. Pour granulated sugar into a medium bowl (we use a cereal bowl for this step) and coat donuts with sugar, 1 at a time. Eat immediately!

Variations

If you don't cut holes in the middle of these donuts, they're great for filling! When the donuts have cooled enough to handle, poke a skewer through the side, going just to the middle of the donut. Fill a pastry bag fitted with a piping tip with Nutella, lemon curd, jam, or whatever you want to fill the donuts with, and squeeze the filling in through the hole you made with the skewer. Fill them before you coat them with sugar.

Maple Spice Cake with Grandma Phyllis's Penuche Frosting

My husband's grandma, Phyllis, lived to be 102. This is one of the few recipes she passed on to her children and grandchildren. Everyone in the family loves the rich, butterscotch frosting, but Grandma's original cake recipe—a relic of the war ration era—was lacking in both taste and texture. For years, I've wanted to remake the cake recipe and give it more sweetness, more flavor, and a lighter, more tender crumb. This revised version, with warm spices to compliment the maple, is a worthy partner for Phyllis's delicious penuche frosting. From now on, nobody will even think about eating the frosting and leaving the cake behind!

Serves 12 to 16

For the cake

- 1 cup butter, softened
- 1 cup brown sugar
- 3/4 cup granulated sugar
- 3 eggs
- 1 teaspoon maple flavoring
- 2 1/4 cups all-purpose flour
- 2 teaspoons cinnamon
- 1/2 teaspoon baking powder
- 1/2 teaspoon baking soda
- 1/2 teaspoon salt
- 1/2 teaspoon nutmeg
- 1/2 teaspoon cloves
- 1 cup buttermilk

For the penuche frosting

- 1 cup brown sugar
- 1/2 cup butter
- 1/4 cup heavy cream
- 2 cups powdered sugar
- Hot water
- 1 cup chopped, toasted pecans or walnuts, optional

continued

1. Preheat oven to 350°F. Spray a 9 x 13-inch cake pan with nonstick baking spray.

2. In a large bowl or in the bowl of a stand mixer, beat butter and both sugars on medium speed until fluffy, about 1 minute. Add eggs and maple flavoring, and beat until smooth, scraping down the sides and bottom of the bowl with a rubber spatula as necessary.

3. In a medium bowl, combine flour, cinnamon, baking powder, baking soda, salt, nutmeg, and cloves. With the mixer on low, add half of the flour mixture, followed by half of the buttermilk. Repeat and mix until smooth.

4. Pour the batter into the cake pan and bake 25–30 minutes, until the top of the cake springs back when lightly pressed, or until a toothpick inserted in the center of the cake comes out clean. Make the frosting while allowing the cake to cool completely.

5. To make the frosting, combine brown sugar and butter in a medium sauce-pan over medium-low heat. Bring to a boil and cook, whisking constantly, for 2 minutes. Whisk in cream and let the mixture return to a boil. Remove the pan from heat and allow to cool to lukewarm, about 30 minutes. Beat in the powdered sugar until the frosting is a smooth, spreadable consistency. If the frosting is too stiff to spread, beat in a little hot water (about a teaspoon at a time) until the frosting reaches a spreadable consistency. Frost the cake immediately and top with chopped nuts if desired.

Pumpkin Bread Pudding with Salted Caramel Sauce

Bread pudding is such a homey, comforting dessert. On chilly nights, I just want to snuggle up on the couch with a big bowl of warm bread pudding smothered in whipped cream. I love the flavors of pumpkin and spice in this particular recipe. They make it so autumnal. It's easy to make but seems fancy, which is a great combo, especially for serving to guests. And I'm going to let you in on a little secret: bread pudding and French toast casserole are essentially the same thing, so feel free to make this for brunch too! **Serves 12**

For the bread pudding

1 large loaf store-bought French bread (about 1 pound), cut into 1-inch cubes (Don't cut off the crusts!)

6 large eggs

1 (15-ounce) can pumpkin purée

1 cup granulated sugar

2 teaspoons vanilla extract

1 teaspoon cinnamon

1/2 teaspoon ginger

1/2 teaspoon salt

1/4 teaspoon cloves

1/4 teaspoon nutmeg

3 cups whole milk

Sweetened whipped cream for topping

For the salted caramel sauce

3/4 cup granulated sugar

1/2 cup water

1/2 cup plus 2 tablespoons heavy cream

5 tablespoons butter

1 teaspoon flaky sea salt or kosher salt

continued

1. Spray a 9 x 13-inch baking dish with nonstick spray. Add the bread cubes.

2. In a large bowl, whisk eggs, pumpkin, sugar, vanilla, cinnamon, ginger, salt, cloves, and nutmeg until very smooth and well combined. Whisk in the milk. Pour the mixture over the bread cubes in the baking dish. Using the back of a large spoon, gently push the bread down to make sure all pieces are wet. Allow to sit for 20 minutes so that the bread can soak up all of the custard.

3. Preheat oven to 350°F. Place a large roasting pan (big enough for your baking dish to fit in) into the oven then put the baking dish in the roasting pan. Carefully pour enough hot water into the roasting pan to reach halfway up the side of the baking dish. DO NOT POUR THE WATER INTO YOUR BREAD PUDDING! Bake 40–45 minutes, until a knife inserted in the middle of the pudding comes out clean.

4. If you can, lift the baking dish out of the roasting pan and set it on a cooling rack. If that will be too tricky, remove the entire roasting pan from the oven very carefully, and then lift out the baking dish. Allow the bread pudding to cool for at least 10 minutes before serving. Serve bread pudding warm, topped with Salted Caramel Sauce and sweetened whipped cream.

5. You can make the caramel sauce while the bread pudding bakes. Combine the sugar and water in a small, heavy-bottom saucepan with tall sides. Heat, stirring constantly until sugar is dissolved, then bring to a boil. Boil until the entire mixture is a light amber color, like the color of clover honey. Stir in the cream. The mixture will sputter, so stand back, and use a long-handled spoon. And I always wear long sleeves and an oven mitt! Remove caramel from heat, and whisk in butter and salt. Allow to cool slightly before serving.

Notes

1. I think leaving the crust on the French bread gives the finished bread pudding a little more substance and structure. Try to cut your bread cubes so that each piece has some crust. If that means making the bread chunks more rectangular than square, that's OK. Just keep them bite-size.

2. Making your own pumpkin purée is easy, and a great project for a fall weekend. Wash, remove seeds, and clean out a small, sweet baking pumpkin, like a Sugar Pie Pumpkin. Cut it in half, brush the fleshy sides lightly with olive oil, and place the cut sides down on a parchment-lined baking sheet. Roast the pumpkin in a 400°F oven for about 45 minutes until tender. Remove from the oven and let cool. Scrape the flesh out of the skin and process it in a food processor until smooth.

The Best Apple Pie

Last year, after an absolutely enormous apple harvest, my husband decided to bake a whole lotta apple pies. He and I took a pie-making class one Saturday morning at our local community college, and it inspired him to perfect his apple pie recipe. So we baked, and baked, and baked, experimenting with crusts and fillings, temperatures and bake times, until we created an apple pie that we both love. Now, homemade apple pies are a little like chocolate chip cookies: everybody has a slightly different idea of what makes them "the best." This particular recipe has a flaky, buttery crust that is pretty easy to whip up, a filling that is soft but not saucy, and spices that are present but not overpowering. It is the best apple pie recipe . . . at our house. **Serves 6 to 8**

For the crust

2 1/2 cups all-purpose flour

1 tablespoon granulated sugar

1 teaspoon salt

12 tablespoons cold butter, cut into chunks

1/2 cup cold shortening, cut into chunks

1 cup ice water (you won't use all of it)

For the filling

3 tablespoons butter

4 pounds apples, peeled, cored, and diced (8 medium apples or 12 cups diced apples

1 cup plus 2 tablespoons granulated sugar

3 tablespoons all-purpose flour

1 tablespoon cornstarch

3/4 teaspoon cinnamon

3/8 teaspoon allspice

3/8 teaspoon salt

1 1/2 tablespoons apple cider vinegar

For the egg wash and sugar topping

1 egg white

1 teaspoon water

Coarse sugar for sprinkling

continued

1. To prepare the crust, combine flour, sugar, and salt in the bowl of a food processor. Pulse a few times to combine. Add the chunks of butter and shortening, and pulse until the mixture resembles coarse corn meal, with a few chunks about the size of peas remaining. Pour just $1/2$ cup of water into a measuring cup (no ice cubes!), add it to the food processor, and pulse until the mixture begins to come together in a single ball of dough. Add small amounts of extra water if needed.

2. Remove the dough from the food processor and divide it in half. Shape each half into a disk about 1-inch thick, and wrap each in plastic wrap. Refrigerate while preparing the filling.

3. Place a baking sheet in the oven and preheat the oven to 425°F.

4. In a large skillet, melt the butter for the filling. Add apples and cook over medium heat, covered, for about 10 minutes, until the apples have released a lot of liquid. Stir occasionally to prevent the apples from sticking to the pan. In a medium bowl, combine sugar, flour, cornstarch, cinnamon, allspice, and salt. Sprinkle the dry ingredients over the apples. Stir to coat and continue cooking the apples until the mixture has thickened, 1–2 minutes more. Remove from heat and stir in vinegar. Spread the filling on a second rimmed baking sheet and put it in the fridge to cool quickly.

5. While the filling cools, finish preparing the crust. Unwrap 1 disk of chilled dough and place it on a floured work surface. Roll it out into a circle about $1/8$ inch thick. Carefully transfer the dough to a 9-inch pie plate. Without stretching the dough, press it into the bottom and up the sides of the pie plate. Roll out the other disk of pie dough to the same thickness.

6. Pour the cooled apple filling into the bottom crust and spread it out in an even layer. Gently place the remaining pie crust over the top of the filling. Trim both crusts so that they only hang over the edge of the pie plate by 1-inch. Fold the extra inch of

dough from both layers under themselves so that the pie crust is sealed and comes just to the edge of the pie plate. Use the tines of a fork to press a decorative pattern into the edge of the crust or use your fingers to pinch the crust edges together. Cut a few small slits in the top crust to allow steam to escape.

7. In a small bowl, whisk egg white with water until well combined. Brush the egg wash over the top crust of the pie then sprinkle with coarse sugar. Place the pie on the preheated baking sheet in the oven. Bake for 15 minutes then reduce the temperature to 350°F and bake 30 more minutes, until the pie is golden. If the edges of the crust start to get too dark, cover them loosely with aluminum foil. Allow the pie to cool before serving.

Variation

I love a single-crust apple pie topped with sweet, buttery streusel every bit as much as I love the classic double-crust version. To make a crumb-topped pie, prepare only half of the recipe for the crust. Instead of putting a second crust on top of the pie, spread the following mixture evenly over the top of the filling right before baking: $1/2$ cup all-purpose flour, $1/3$ cup brown sugar, 1 teaspoon cinnamon, $1/4$ teaspoon salt, and 5 tablespoons melted butter. Combine those 5 ingredients in a medium bowl, and use your hands to mix them, pressing chunks together and then letting them crumble back into the bowl, until well combined. The baking time and temperature are the same.

winter

WINTER AT THE FARMHOUSE is a quiet season, a time to say goodbye to the past year, to ponder and plan for a new season, and to rest and recharge for the year ahead. We put our garden to bed with a layer of compost and fall leaves that will turn into fertile soil for spring seeds. We've harvested and preserved as much of the summer and fall bounty as we can; it's time now to enjoy the fruits of all our hard work.

There's a fire going in the fireplace, and a basket full of quilts and blankets in the corner of the living room. When we're lucky enough to get a snow day, we sled and build snowmen, and watch the chickens and bunnies try to navigate their new winter wonderland. We bake bread and holiday treats to deliver to neighbors. We work on projects like homemade candles and crocheted scarves. We are all tucked in and cozy for the next few months, awaiting a new year and another spring, when we will start the cycle again.

Farmhouse Weekends in Winter

tap sugar maples • dip beeswax candles • cut down your own Christmas tree

• take a horse-drawn sleigh ride • sip hot cocoa from a thermos

• go sledding • make maple candy • knit a pair of cozy socks

• make a batch of soap from scratch • bake and eat a pan of monkey bread

Baked Oatmeal with Brown Butter, Apples & Pecans

Many years ago, I stumbled upon a recipe for baked oatmeal from Heidi Swanson's book, Super Natural Every Day. *I'd never heard of baked oatmeal before (although there are a million and one variations now), but as an oatmeal fan, I was intrigued. It was every bit as delicious and wholesome and comforting as I dreamed it would be, and baked oatmeal has become a family favorite in the nearly ten years since. Depending on what fresh, frozen, or dried fruits you mix in, it is great for any season, but its warm, nourishing goodness makes it especially wonderful in the winter. This is my favorite version, filled with toasted pecans and tart apples, and topped with real maple syrup. Don't skip that luxurious drizzle of cream at the end; it makes the oatmeal just a little naughty, but in the best possible way!* **Serves 5 to 6**

1/2 cup chopped pecans

4 tablespoons butter, plus more for buttering the baking dish

2 cups old-fashioned rolled oats

1 1/2 cups peeled, cored, and small diced apple (about 1 medium apple)

1/3 cup lightly packed brown sugar

1 1/2 teaspoons ground cinnamon

1 teaspoon baking powder

3/8 teaspoon salt

2 cups whole milk

2 teaspoons vanilla extract

1 egg

Heavy cream and pure maple syrup, for serving

continued

1. Preheat oven to 375°F.

2. Once the oven is preheated, place the chopped pecans on a rimmed baking sheet, and toast until fragrant, 5–7 minutes. Watch carefully so they don't burn. Set aside to cool.

3. Place the butter in a small skillet over medium-low heat. Cook, stirring gently, until the butter is melted and the solids in the bottom have turned golden brown, about 5 minutes. Remove from heat and set aside to cool.

4. Generously butter an 8 x 8-inch baking pan or 2-quart baking dish.

5. In a medium bowl, combine rolled oats, apple, brown sugar, cinnamon, baking powder, salt, and toasted pecans. Add browned butter and toss. In a medium bowl or large measuring cup, combine milk, vanilla, and egg. Whisk until combined then add to the dry ingredients and stir until well mixed.

6. Pour the oatmeal mixture into the buttered pan and spread it into an even layer. Bake for 35–40 minutes until the oatmeal looks golden and set.

7. Serve hot with heavy cream and maple syrup for drizzling on top.

Variations & Notes

1. Use an apple variety that has a good balance of sweet and tart, like pink lady or Honeycrisp.

2. Stir 1 1/2 cups fresh berries (whatever you love that is in season) into the oatmeal mixture in place of the apples. My family loves fresh blueberries, and I'm partial to blackberries. I've even mixed both blackberries and apples in.

3. Chopped nuts are finicky things and can burn really easily. And every oven is slightly different. Keep a close eye on those nuts, and if they start to brown before your timer goes off, feel free to pull them out of the oven early.

Cinnamon-Sugar Monkey Bread

My mother-in-law makes an amazing all-purpose enriched dough. Its most frequent incarnation is as dinner rolls for family gatherings, holidays, birthdays, etc. But it's also my go-to dough for cinnamon rolls, sticky buns, orange rolls, and our family's favorite snowy day treat: monkey bread. We don't get snow days very often here in western Oregon, but when we do, by golly, we sled down our hill, build snowmen, and make Momo's monkey bread! With balls of dough dipped in melted butter and rolled in cinnamon sugar then nestled in all the nooks and crannies of a Bundt pan and baked until hot and fluffy, it is basically just like heaven. **Makes 1 Bundt pan or about 8 servings**

For the dough

1/4 cup warm water

1 tablespoon active dry yeast

1 cup warm milk (microwaved for about 1 minute)

1/3 cup granulated sugar

1/3 cup butter, melted (microwaved for about 1 minute)

1 teaspoon salt

1 egg

4 cups all-purpose flour

For the cinnamon coating

1 cup granulated sugar

2 tablespoons ground cinnamon

6 tablespoons butter, melted and cooled slightly

For the cream cheese drizzle

2 ounces cream cheese, softened

2 tablespoons butter, softened

A splash of vanilla extract

A pinch of salt

1 cup powdered sugar

Whole milk

continued

1. To make the bread dough, combine the warm water and yeast in a small bowl or glass measuring cup. Set aside in a warm spot for 10 minutes until the yeast is activated and the mixture begins to grow in volume. Meanwhile, combine the warm milk, sugar, melted butter, salt, and egg in a large bowl or in the bowl of a stand mixer. Add the proofed yeast mixture and mix to combine. Add the flour. If you are using a stand mixer, switch to the dough hook attachment at this point. If you are making the bread dough in a large bowl, stir it with a wooden spoon until it gets too difficult then use your hands. Either way, knead the dough for 5 minutes until smooth and elastic. At this point, the dough might still be slightly sticky, and that's OK. Place the dough in a bowl that's been sprayed with nonstick baking spray or lightly coated with oil, cover it with a damp towel, and set in a warm place to rise until doubled in volume, about 1 hour.

2. Spray a standard Bundt pan well with nonstick baking spray and set aside. When the dough has doubled in volume, turn it out onto a well-floured work surface, and knead it for about 1 minute. Divide the dough into 36 equal portions. Combine the sugar and cinnamon in a small bowl. Dip a small ball of dough in melted butter then roll it in cinnamon sugar and place it in the Bundt pan. Repeat with all the dough pieces. Cover the pan with a damp towel and place it in a warm spot to rise for another 30 minutes.

3. Preheat oven to 350°F for regular pans and 325°F for black or dark pans. When the monkey bread has risen, remove the towel and bake the bread for 25–30 minutes until it is golden on top. If you have a digital food thermometer, the internal temperature should be 190°F. Remove the monkey bread from the oven, allow it to cool for 10 minutes, and then flip it over onto a serving plate or cake stand, remove the pan, and allow the monkey bread to cool while you make the Cream Cheese Drizzle.

4. Combine the cream cheese, butter, vanilla, and salt in a medium bowl and beat until well mixed. Add the powdered sugar and beat until it's as smooth as you can get it. Whisk in milk, a little at a time, until the mixture has a thick but drizzleable consistency. Using a spoon, drizzle the cream cheese mixture over the monkey bread. Eat immediately!

Bakery-Style Cranberry-Orange Muffins

What makes a "bakery-style" muffin? For me, a bakery-style muffin must be impressively tall, with a top that hangs well over the top of the pan and forms a deliciously crispy edge. These cranberry-orange muffins are perfect bakery-style specimens: tall and tender, lightly sweet and citrusy, with a crunchy sugar coating on top that is quite irresistible. They're a favorite during the holiday season when fresh cranberries are easy to find at the grocery store. And if you buy a few extra bags of cranberries and pop them in the freezer, you can enjoy cranberry-orange muffins for breakfast all year long!

Makes 12 generous muffins

1 cup granulated sugar

1 large orange, zested

2 1/2 cups all-purpose flour

1 tablespoon baking powder

1 teaspoon baking soda

1/2 teaspoon salt

1 cup buttermilk

2 eggs

1/2 cup butter, melted

1 1/2 cups fresh or frozen cranberries, chopped into quarters

2 tablespoons coarse sugar

1. Preheat oven to 375°F. Generously spray a standard 12-cup muffin tin with nonstick baking spray, being sure to get the top of the pan as well.

2. In a large bowl, combine sugar and orange zest. Rub the zest and sugar together with your fingers until the mixture is very fragrant and has the consistency of wet sand. Add the flour, baking powder, baking soda, and salt to the bowl and stir to combine.

3. In a medium bowl or in a large glass measuring cup, combine buttermilk and eggs until well mixed. Add the buttermilk mixture to the dry ingredients and stir gently until mostly

combined. Add the melted butter and stir just until smooth. Fold the cranberries gently into the muffin batter.

4. Divide the batter evenly among the cups in the muffin tin. You will use all the batter, which means the cups will be very full. Sprinkle $1/2$ teaspoon coarse sugar on top of each muffin.

5. Bake for 20-25 minutes, until golden on the edges and a skewer inserted in the middle of a muffin comes out clean. Allow to cool in the pan for 5 minutes then gently remove the muffins from the pan and set them on a wire rack to cool completely.

Note

These muffins are best fresh, but they're actually quite good leftover too. Store any leftovers in an airtight container and eat them within 2 days of baking.

Fluffy Farm-Style Biscuits with Sausage Gravy

Homemade biscuits smothered in savory sausage gravy make an appearance on our breakfast table often, especially when we get together with grandparents, uncles and aunts, or cousins. My husband's whole side of the family requests biscuits and gravy for breakfast on Christmas morning as part of what they call a "farmer's breakfast," and not a family reunion goes by that biscuits don't pop up on the menu. In addition to being absolutely delicious topped with sausage gravy, these buttermilk biscuits are fantastic slathered with butter and jam or copious amounts of honey butter. And if eight biscuits aren't enough, you can easily double the recipe! **Makes 8 biscuits and enough gravy to cover them generously**

For the biscuits

2 cups all-purpose flour

2 1/2 teaspoons baking powder

1/2 teaspoon salt

6 tablespoons cold butter, cut into small pieces

3/4 cup buttermilk

2 tablespoons butter, melted

For the gravy

1 pound bulk pork sausage

1/4 cup chopped scallions, white and light green parts (about 1/2 a bunch)

1 tablespoon butter

1/4 cup all-purpose flour

1 teaspoon ground sage

3 cups whole milk

Salt and pepper to taste

continued

1. Preheat oven to 425°F. Line a baking sheet with parchment paper.

2. In the bowl of a food processor, combine flour, baking powder, and salt; process for a few seconds just to combine. Add cold butter chunks and pulse about 10 times until the butter starts to be incorporated into the dry ingredients. Add the buttermilk, and continue pulsing the mixture until the dough begins to stick together in clumps.

3. Turn the dough out onto a floured counter, and press it together into one mass. Using a rolling pin, roll it into a rectangle about $1/2$ inch thick. Fold one of the short sides down then the other short side up, like folding a business letter. Turn the dough so that the open side is facing you. Roll the dough out again into a rectangle about $1/2$ inch thick, and again, fold it like a letter. Turn it again so that the open side is facing you, and roll it out one more time. This time, only roll it to a thickness of $3/4$ inch. Use a $2 1/2$-inch biscuit cutter to cut rounds. Place the rounds—very close together but not touching—on the prepared baking sheet. Pile up dough scraps, reroll them, and cut out more biscuits. Continue until you've used up all the dough. I usually only reroll the scraps once, and make the very last scraps into a very ugly biscuit that still tastes delicious!

4. Brush the tops of the biscuits with melted butter. Bake the biscuits for 15–18 minutes until tall and golden. Brush the biscuits with another coat of melted butter.

5. While the biscuits are baking, make the sausage gravy. Crumble sausage into a large skillet, and cook over medium heat until no longer pink inside and nicely browned outside. When the sausage has cooked for a few minutes and the fat has started to render, add the scallions. Drain off and discard any excess grease. Add butter to the skillet and allow it to melt. Sprinkle flour and sage on the meat and stir until flour is absorbed, about 1 minute. Add milk and simmer, stirring frequently, until thickened, about 5 minutes. Salt and pepper to taste. Serve over warm biscuits.

Notes

1. The folding technique this biscuit recipe calls for is called a "letter fold." It's used in making flaky pastries like croissants and is what gives these biscuits so many buttery layers. You can make buttermilk biscuits without doing the letter folds, but they really only take a couple of extra minutes and make the biscuits much, much taller!

2. When cutting the biscuits, don't push the biscuit cutter down and then twist it. Just push it straight down and lift the biscuits out.

3. If we're having these biscuits without the gravy, I usually make a batch and a half. The ingredients still fit in my food processor just fine, and we get 12 delicious biscuits to enjoy with jam or honey butter. To make homemade honey butter, combine equal parts honey and softened, room temperature butter. Mix with a spoon until smooth.

4. My family is very divided on this issue, but I like to sprinkle my biscuits and gravy with very thinly sliced green onions (the darker parts that you didn't use to make the gravy). I think it adds a pop of color and fresh onion zing.

Honeyed Citrus Salad

I've always been a citrus girl. I love how citrus fruits smell, how they look, and most of all, how they taste, which is like sunshine in the deep midwinter. I think it's positively providential that citrus season peaks in the darkest, coldest months. It's like a little gift. This salad is a celebration of winter citrus fruits—a big bowl of sunshine! You can use any combination of sweet citrus fruits that you like. Use whatever your local store is stocking. **Serves 8**

4 tablespoons honey

3 tablespoons Meyer lemon juice (from 1 to 2 medium Meyer lemons)

1 teaspoon Meyer lemon zest (from 1 to 2 medium Meyer lemons)

$1/2$ teaspoon vanilla extract

8 pieces large citrus fruit (Cara Cara oranges, Valencia oranges, blood oranges, grapefruits, tangerines, etc.)

1 cup honey-flavored Greek yogurt

1 cup granola (I like ginger or honey-flavored granolas best)

1. In a small bowl, combine honey, lemon juice, zest, and vanilla. Whisk until smooth; set aside.

2. Cut the peel off the citrus fruit, and cut each fruit crosswise into slices about $1/4$ inch thick then cut each slice into 4 or 6 pieces to make bite-size chunks. Place the fruit in a large, clear bowl, and pour the honey-lemon mixture over the top. Toss gently. Chill until ready to serve.

3. Before serving, gently toss the salad again. Serve with honey-flavored yogurt and granola for topping.

Notes

1. If you can't find Meyer lemons, you can use regular lemons instead.

2. Smaller citrus fruits work just as well as large ones. If you use clementines, Mandarins, or even small blood oranges, just use twice as many.

Loaded Home Fries

A note before diving in: you have to bake the potatoes the night before and then refrigerate them. It's not a lot of work, but it is important to the final outcome of these amazing breakfast potatoes. Now that we have that out of the way, these potatoes make breakfast an event. They're fluffy on the inside, brown and crispy on the outside, and perfectly seasoned. But that's not the end of this potato story! They're then covered with classic potato toppings: salty bacon, savory green onions, cool sour cream, and a generous helping of melted cheddar cheese. It takes them from delicious to out-of-this-world. A huge thank you goes to our friend Jared for sharing the cold baked potato trick with me!

Makes 4 to 6 servings

2 pounds russet potatoes (2 to 4 potatoes depending on their size)

2 tablespoons extra virgin olive oil

2 tablespoons butter

Seasoned salt

Freshly ground black pepper

2 cups grated cheddar cheese

8 slices bacon, cooked and crumbled

1 bunch green onions, finely chopped, white and light green parts only

Sour cream

1. Preheat oven to 425°F.

2. Scrub the potatoes until they're clean then dry them off with a kitchen towel.

3. Prick the potatoes all over with a fork to allow steam to escape while they're baking. Wrap each potato in aluminum foil, place on a baking sheet or just right into the oven, and bake until tender, about 1 hour.

4. Remove from the oven, allow to cool to room temperature, then refrigerate overnight. Don't worry about unwrapping them.

5. In a large skillet (preferably nonstick), combine olive oil and butter over medium heat. Unwrap and dice cold potatoes. Add potatoes to the skillet, season liberally with seasoned salt and pepper, and toss gently to coat with oil and butter. Spread the potatoes out as much as you can in an even layer (you want as many potatoes touching the skillet as possible), and allow to cook undisturbed for 10 minutes. Toss the potatoes gently and continue to cook until brown on several sides and heated through, another 5 minutes. Add more seasoned salt and pepper to taste.

6. Sprinkle cheese on top, remove from heat, and cover the skillet with the lid (or a piece of foil) slightly askew just until the cheese melts. Serve immediately with bacon, green onions, and sour cream for topping.

Pop's Perfect Buttermilk Pancakes

These pancakes will make anyone into a pancake fan! Believe it or not, I wasn't very fond of pancakes when I was growing up, but my father-in-law's pancakes changed my mind forever. I think he makes them with buttermilk and magic because I could eat them all the time. Anytime someone suggests we have Pop's pancakes, whether it is for breakfast on a rainy Sunday morning or dinner on a hectic weeknight, I'm always an early and enthusiastic supporter. These pancakes are light and fluffy, never, ever dense or—heaven forbid—chewy, and they taste simply amazing, so much so that more than one person has uttered the phrase, "Oh my gosh, these are the best pancakes I've ever eaten!" after their first bite.

Makes about 24 (5-inch) pancakes

2 cups all-purpose flour

1 rounded tablespoon baking powder

1 tablespoon granulated sugar

1 teaspoon baking soda

1/2 teaspoon salt

4 eggs

1/2 cup vegetable or canola oil

1 quart buttermilk

Softened butter and maple syrup for serving

1. Preheat a nonstick griddle pan or shallow skillet over medium-low heat.

2. In a large bowl, combine flour, baking powder, sugar, baking soda, and salt. Put eggs and oil in a large glass measuring cup, and add enough buttermilk to make 1 quart of wet ingredients. Whisk to combine then pour the wet ingredients into the dry ingredients and whisk until smooth.

3. Scoop the batter using a 1/4-cup measuring cup onto the griddle. Each scoop of batter will make 1 (5-inch) pancake. Cook the pancakes

without flipping them until the bubbles coming up to the surface of the batter and popping have slowed down and the batter looks slightly drier on top, about 2–3 minutes, then flip. The pancakes should be golden on the bottom. Cook 1–2 minutes more until the other side of each pancake is also golden then stack on a warm plate next to the stove and continue cooking more pancakes. Serve immediately with butter and syrup.

Note

We often add extras to these pancakes, usually sprinkling something on each pancake right after pouring the batter on the griddle and before flipping. Mini chocolate chips, fresh or thawed berries, diced summer peaches, and even sweet corn and scallions taste great!

Creamy Potato-Leek Soup

Leeks are one of the gifts of a winter garden. If your winters are mild, you can leave them in the ground until you need them, and if your winters are harsh, you can store them or even chop, wash, and freeze them to use through the cold, dark months. This soup, full of delicate leek and hearty potato flavors, is a smooth and satisfying end to a winter day. **Serves 6 to 8**

3 large leeks (just under 2 pounds before being trimmed)

4 tablespoons butter, divided

3 cloves garlic, grated or finely minced

6 cups chicken or vegetable broth

2 pounds Yukon Gold potatoes, peeled and diced

2 large sprigs fresh thyme

1 bay leaf

$1/2$ teaspoon salt

A big pinch of freshly ground black pepper

1 cup heavy cream

Crispy, crumbled bacon, minced chives, and sour cream for serving (optional)

1. Cut off and discard the root end and dark green leaves of the leeks. Cut the leeks in half lengthwise then crosswise in $1/4$-inch sections. Put the chopped leeks in a large bowl and cover with cold water. Swish the leeks around in the water to remove any dirt. Using a slotted spoon or just your hands, scoop out the clean leeks and pile them up on a clean kitchen towel to drain.

2. In a large Dutch oven or soup pot over low heat, melt 3 tablespoons butter. Add the chopped leeks and garlic and stir to coat with butter. Cover and cook until the leeks are very tender but not at all brown, 10–15 minutes.

3. Add broth, diced potatoes, thyme, bay leaf, salt, and pepper. Increase the heat to bring the soup to a boil.

Reduce the heat to keep the soup just above a simmer, and cook, stirring occasionally, until potatoes are very tender, 15–20 minutes.

4. Turn off the heat, remove the thyme sprigs and bay leaf, and purée the soup with an immersion blender until smooth and velvety.

5. Add cream and remaining butter, and turn the heat back on if necessary to bring the soup up to a steaming temperature. Salt and pepper to taste, and serve with or without toppings.

Note

You can use a regular blender to purée the soup, but you'll have to work in batches. Only fill your blender jar halfway, put the lid on slightly askew, and hold it in place with a kitchen towel to let steam escape while not burning yourself.

Garlic Butter & Parmesan Roasted Winter Veggies

Roasting veggies then topping them with garlic butter and nutty Parmesan cheese is just the best way to eat vegetables, plain and simple. This recipe focuses on hearty winter veggies like cauliflower, squash, and Brussels sprouts, but the same process works for basically any vegetable at any time of year—you just have to adjust the time. **Serves 6 to 8**

1 large head cauliflower, cut into bite-size florets

1 delicata squash, halved, seeds removed, and cut into $1/2$-inch-thick crescents

10 ounces Brussels sprouts, trimmed and halved (12–15 Brussels sprouts)

3 tablespoons olive oil

Heaping $1/2$ teaspoon kosher salt

Freshly ground black pepper

2 tablespoons butter

2 cloves garlic

$1/4$ cup finely grated Parmesan cheese

1 tablespoon chopped fresh parsley

1. Preheat oven to 425°F. Line a baking sheet with parchment paper. Spread the prepared vegetables out in an even layer on the baking sheet. Drizzle with olive oil, and sprinkle with salt and pepper. Use your hands to gently toss the veggies until they are all evenly coated with oil and seasoning. Roast the veggies in the oven for 15–20 minutes until everything is tender.

2. While the veggies are roasting, melt the butter in a small saucepan over low heat. When the butter is melted, grate the garlic into the butter using a microplane grater. Allow the garlic and butter to continue cooking until the garlic just begins to turn golden, about 10 minutes. Remove from heat and set aside.

3. When the veggies are tender, pour the garlic butter over them, and toss gently with a wooden spoon or spatula until the garlic butter is evenly distributed. Sprinkle evenly with Parmesan cheese and parsley, and serve immediately.

Variations

You can really use any combination of winter vegetables that you want. If you don't like Brussels sprouts or cauliflower or squash, feel free to leave that one out and substitute with an equal amount of something else. Altogether, you need about 2 pounds of vegetables.

Lemon-Herb Chicken Thighs with Roasted Fingerling Potatoes

I'm in love with boneless, skinless chicken thighs, and I'm not afraid to admit it! They are less prone to overcooking than chicken breasts, and they have great flavor. In this—dare I say elegant!—one-pan dinner, they're paired with buttery fingerling potatoes (the more colorful the better), flavorful herbs, and tart lemons. The chicken thighs and potatoes soak up the flavors of the lemons and herbs, plus a splash of white wine at the end, to produce a truly tasty dinner. And thanks to the lemon slices that roast on top, it's also easy on the eyes. **Serves 6**

2 tablespoons extra virgin olive oil

1 1/2 pounds fingerling potatoes, halved or quartered, depending on size (about 16 fingerling potatoes)

Kosher salt

Freshly ground black pepper

3 pounds boneless, skinless chicken thighs

2 teaspoons bottled minced garlic

1 teaspoon fresh thyme leaves

1/2 teaspoon dried oregano

A splash of white wine

2 lemons, cut into 1/4-inch slices

1. Preheat oven to 425°F.

2. In a large, oven-safe skillet or Dutch oven, heat olive oil over medium heat. I use a 14-inch cast iron skillet. If you don't have anything that big, use 2 smaller skillets. Add quartered potatoes and season with a pinch of salt and pepper. Cook potatoes for 10 minutes, stirring every 2–3 minutes.

3. Dry off the chicken thighs with paper towels then season lightly with salt and pepper. Clear space in the pan for the chicken thighs so that they can touch the bottom of the pan. If the bottom of the pan looks dry, add another drizzle of

continued

oil. Add the chicken thighs, top side down, and allow to cook for 5 minutes undisturbed.

4. While the chicken cooks, combine garlic, thyme, and oregano in a small bowl; set aside.

5. After 5 minutes, flip the chicken thighs over. Sprinkle garlic mixture and another pinch of salt and pepper over the chicken and potatoes. Add a splash of white wine to the pan, and lay lemon slices evenly over the top of everything. Drizzle lemon slices lightly with olive oil.

6. Place the skillet or Dutch oven in the oven and roast, uncovered, until potatoes are tender and chicken has reached an internal temperature of 170°F, about 10–15 minutes. Remove from the oven, press the lemon slices with the back of a spoon to release their juice, and serve immediately.

Note

Freshly minced garlic sounds like such a good idea in this dish, right? In my experience, preminced garlic from a jar is much better in this recipe. Fresh garlic reacts with fresh lemon juice and turns a bright shade of turquoise, which doesn't affect the flavor of the dish at all, but looks very strange and kind of unappetizing. Minced garlic from a jar doesn't react that way!

Mom's Pan-Fried Chicken Tenders

My mom's fried chicken is one of my favorite dinners in the whole, wide world. It gets requested often for special Sunday suppers and birthday dinners. It's savory and comforting, and surprisingly easy to make. Instead of deep-frying bone-in chicken pieces, my mom has always pan-fried boneless chicken breast tenders. The result is a juicy, flavorful chicken dinner that cooks through in less than 15 minutes. I think it will undoubtedly become a favorite in your family too.

Makes 6 servings

Vegetable or canola oil

2 eggs

2 tablespoons water

2 cups all-purpose flour

2 teaspoons paprika

2 teaspoons onion powder

2 teaspoons garlic powder

2 1/2 teaspoons salt

1/2 teaspoon black pepper

2 1/2 to 3 pounds boneless, skinless chicken breast tenders

1. Pour enough oil into a large, nonstick skillet to cover the entire bottom of the pan. Set over medium heat.

2. In a shallow dish or pie plate, whisk the eggs and water together until well combined. Combine the flour and all seasonings in a medium container with a tight-fitting lid.

3. Working in batches, coat the chicken tenders in the egg mixture, shake off any excess egg mixture, then place in the container of seasoned flour. Tightly close the container, and shake gently to thoroughly coat the chicken tenders with flour.

continued

4. Place the coated chicken tenders in the skillet, and cook until golden on the bottom, about 7–8 minutes. Flip the chicken tenders over, and continue to cook until golden on the other side, another 5–7 minutes. If you have a reliable food thermometer, the temperature of the chicken should be 170°F when it is cooked all the way through.

5. Remove fried chicken from the pan, place on a plate or serving platter lined with paper towels, and serve hot.

Notes

1. If I'm making the full recipe, I either have 2 skillets going at the same time, or I have to cook 2 batches in the same skillet, 1 after the other. I usually do the latter and just tell people to come get their food when it's hot, and we eat in shifts. It's not ideal for a formal, sit-down dinner, but that way everybody gets piping hot, crispy chicken, and I don't mind chatting with the eaters while I stand at the stove frying up another batch of chicken tenders.

2. Your first instinct might be to use tongs to turn the chicken over and to get it out of the skillet when it is done cooking, but I find that tongs have a tendency to rip up the crispy coating on the chicken. I use a thin, metal spatula instead. No crispy coating breakage!

Tangy Buttermilk Coleslaw

Coleslaw is one of my go-to side dishes. We think of it as a summer side that goes perfectly with barbecue, but it's use of pantry staples and cold-weather veggies make it great for winter too. And the flavors can add a much-needed zing of freshness to a season when foods tend to get heavy. I never buy premade coleslaw dressing because this homemade version is super simple to make and tastes so good. It has the perfect balance of sweetness and tanginess that makes coleslaw so delicious, and uses ingredients that are easy to find and probably already in your refrigerator and pantry. This coleslaw recipe is also great for serving to guests because it actually tastes best when it is made ahead of time and chilled for several hours. **Makes 8 to 10 servings**

8 cups finely chopped cabbage (1 1/2 to 2 pounds)

1/4 cup shredded carrot

1/2 cup mayonnaise

1/3 cup granulated sugar

1/4 cup milk

1/4 cup buttermilk

1/4 cup apple cider vinegar

1/2 teaspoon salt

Freshly ground black pepper

1. Mix cabbage and carrots in a very large bowl and set aside.

2. Combine the remaining ingredients in a medium bowl and whisk vigorously until smooth. Pour the dressing over the cabbage mixture and toss to coat. Cover and refrigerate 2–3 hours before serving.

Note

A food processor fitted with a shredding disk makes quick work of the cabbage and carrots.

(Almost) No-Bake
Meyer Lemon Cream Tart

Lemon curd is so luxurious that it surely must be hard to make, right? It's actually a breeze to whip up; it can be done start to finish in less than 20 minutes. After you make your first batch, I think you'll start looking for more and more excuses to make it. In the late winter months when beautifully floral Meyer lemons are in season, this tart is an exceptional use of Meyer lemon curd. Bonus points for a simple press-in crust and a four-ingredient filling! **Serves 8**

For the crust

1 1/4 cups all-purpose flour

1/2 cup powdered sugar

1/4 teaspoon salt

1/2 cup butter, softened

For the Meyer lemon curd

3 egg yolks

1 whole egg

1/2 cup granulated sugar

1/3 cup fresh Meyer lemon juice
(from about 3 large Meyer lemons)

2 tablespoons Meyer lemon zest

A pinch of salt

2 tablespoons butter,
cut into chunks

For the cream cheese layer

1/2 cup heavy whipping cream

1/3 cup granulated sugar

8 ounces cream cheese, room
temperature and cut into chunks

1/2 teaspoon vanilla extract

Lightly sweetened whipped
cream for serving

continued

1. To make the crust, preheat oven to 350°F. Combine the flour, powdered sugar, and salt in a large bowl or in the bowl of a stand mixer. Add the butter, and beat until the mixture looks sandy and there are no large chunks of butter remaining. Press the mixture into the bottom and up the sides of a 9-inch tart pan with a removable bottom. It's helpful to use a small, flat-bottomed measuring cup or drinking cup to press the mixture into the pan neatly. Bake the crust for 20 minutes until golden. Cool completely before filling.

2. To make the Meyer lemon curd, combine egg yolks, whole egg, sugar, Meyer lemon juice, zest, and a pinch of salt in an nonreactive pan. Whisk constantly over medium heat until the mixture thickens to a pudding-like consistency, about 3 minutes. Remove from heat and press through a mesh sieve into a medium bowl. Add the butter, and stir until melted and incorporated. Place a piece of plastic wrap, parchment paper, or waxed paper directly on the surface of the curd, and refrigerate it until completely chilled.

3. To make the cream cheese layer, beat cream and sugar in a medium bowl until stiff peaks form. With the mixer on low, add softened cream cheese, little by little, and beat until smooth. Beat in the vanilla.

4. To assemble the tart, spread cream cheese mixture evenly in the bottom of the cooled crust. Top with lemon curd. Chill for at least 2 hours then serve topped with whipped cream.

Notes & Variations

1. Meyer lemons are sweet and delicious, with yummy floral notes, but they aren't available all year. Regular old lemons will make a perfectly acceptable substitute!

2. When you first add the cream cheese to the whipped cream when making the filling, the mixture will look curdled and chunky, and you'll probably worry that you've ruined it. Don't panic! Just keep beating the mixture, and it will get smooth and fluffy.

3. If you don't have a tart pan, never fear! Just use a standard 9-inch pie pan instead. You won't be able to pop the whole tart out for serving, but it will still be delicious. You'll just have to serve it straight from the pie pan like you would any other pie.

Homestyle Chocolate Cake

I love making cakes that you can just serve out of the pan. They taste every bit as delicious as fancy-looking cakes, but are so much easier to make. This classic chocolate cake is a perfect weekend dessert, and makes a great birthday cake too! I'm sharing all of our favorite frosting recipes so you can choose your favorite combo. **Serves 12 to 16**

2 cups all-purpose flour

1/2 cup natural cocoa powder (not Dutch-processed), like Hershey's

2 teaspoons baking soda

1 teaspoon salt

2 cups granulated sugar

1/2 cup butter, softened

2 eggs

2 teaspoons vanilla extract

2 cups strong, hot coffee

1. Preheat oven to 350°F. Spray a 9 x 13-inch baking pan with nonstick cooking spray.

2. In a medium bowl, combine flour, cocoa powder, baking soda, and salt; set aside.

3. In a large bowl or in the bowl of a stand mixer, cream the sugar and butter on medium speed until light and fluffy, about 2 minutes. Add the eggs and vanilla and beat until smooth. With the mixer running on low, add half of the dry ingredients to the wet ingredients, and mix until just combined. Add half of the hot coffee by slowly pouring it down the inside of the bowl. Make sure it doesn't splash out! Add the rest of the dry ingredients and the rest of the coffee in the same manner. Beat until smooth.

continued

4. Pour the batter, which will be very liquidy, into the cake pan, and bake until a toothpick inserted in the center comes out clean, 30–35 minutes. Allow the cake to cool completely before frosting.

Notes & Variations

1. For Chocolate Frosting: Combine 3 cups powdered sugar, 12 tablespoons softened butter, 3 ounces unsweetened chocolate, melted, 3 tablespoons heavy cream, $1^1/2$ teaspoons vanilla extract, and a pinch of salt. Beat until smooth and silky. Stir it a few times with a wooden spoon or rubber spatula to remove large air bubbles.

2. For Peanut Butter Frosting: Beat $1/2$ cup peanut butter, $1/2$ cup softened butter, $1/2$ teaspoon vanilla extract, and a pinch of salt until smooth. Beat in $1/2$ pound powdered sugar and $2^1/2$ tablespoons heavy cream alternately until everything is mixed in then turn the mixer up to high and beat the frosting for 2–3 minutes until it is very smooth and fluffy. Stir it a few times with a wooden spoon or rubber spatula to remove large air bubbles.

3. For Vanilla Frosting: Combine 1 pound powdered sugar, $1/2$ cup softened butter, 4 tablespoons heavy cream (even just milk will do), 1 teaspoon vanilla extract, and a pinch of salt. Beat until smooth and fluffy. Stir it a few times with a wooden spoon or rubber spatula to remove large air bubbles.

4. For Cream Cheese Frosting, see page 45. You can even use the citrus-flavored cream cheese frosting on page 48 if you love the flavors of orange and chocolate together! Just double the recipe so you have enough to frost the entire 9 x 13-inch cake.

5. This chocolate cake recipe also makes delicious cupcakes! Spray 2 cupcake pans with nonstick baking spray or line them with paper liners, divide the batter evenly among the 24 cups, and bake for 18–20 minutes.

Old-Fashioned Oatmeal Cake with Broiled Coconut-Pecan Topping

The name of this recipe really says it all. It is the quintessential old-fashioned cake recipe that doesn't even require a mixer, just a good wooden spoon, and lots of the ingredients are pantry staples. This is the kind of cake you'd make if you got to bring dessert to Sunday dinner at Grandma's house. The flavors are simple and comforting, but the broiled coconut-pecan topping is sweet and sinfully good, and makes the whole thing taste special. Thanks to our friends Emily and Jared for sharing it with us! **Serves 12**

For the cake

1 cup old-fashioned rolled oats

1/2 cup butter

1 1/2 cups boiling water

1 cup brown sugar

1 cup granulated sugar

2 eggs

1 teaspoon vanilla extract

1 1/3 cups all-purpose flour

1 teaspoon baking soda

1 teaspoon cinnamon

1/2 teaspoon nutmeg

1/2 teaspoon salt

For the topping

1/2 cup butter

1/2 cup granulated sugar

1/4 cup cream or evaporated milk

1 teaspoon vanilla extract

A pinch of salt

1 cup sweetened coconut flakes

1 cup chopped pecans

continued

1. Preheat the oven to 350°F. Lightly grease a 9 x 13-inch baking dish.

2. Put oats and butter in a large bowl, and pour boiling water over the top. Allow to sit, stirring occasionally, until butter is melted.

3. Stir in both sugars. Add eggs and vanilla, and stir until combined.

4. In a medium bowl, combine flour, baking soda, cinnamon, nutmeg, and salt. Add the dry ingredients to the oat mixture, and stir until combined. Pour the batter into the baking dish and bake until a toothpick inserted in the center comes out clean, 30–35 minutes.

5. While the cake bakes, prepare the topping. In a medium saucepan, melt butter. When the butter is melted, stir in sugar, cream, vanilla, and salt. Stir until smooth then add coconut and pecans.

6. When the cake is done baking, take it out of the oven, turn the oven to the broil setting, and move the rack to the highest spot. Spread the topping evenly over the top of the hot cake, put the cake back in the oven, and broil for 1–2 minutes until the coconut is golden. Watch the topping very carefully to make sure it doesn't burn! Remove the cake and allow it to cool before serving.

Note

Our friends think this cake tastes best with half the amount of topping, but my sweet tooth and I like the full topping recipe.

Sticky Toffee Gingerbread Cake

This cake is so everything. It's so holiday-ish, so wintery, so old-fashioned, so comforting, and, of course, so tasty. There are a million different recipes for gingerbread cake. Some are dark and dense and full of blackstrap molasses and almost pungent spices. But my favorite gingerbread cakes are sweet instead of bitter, warm instead of harsh. The sticky toffee sauce spooned over squares of this cake is luxuriously smooth and rich, and the lightly sweetened whipped cream lifts all the heavy, winter flavors into the light. This cake is simple enough for a quiet night in after a day of playing in the snow, but rich enough to be a celebration cake at any and all winter-time festivities. **Serves 6 to 8**

For the cake

- 6 tablespoons butter, softened
- 2/3 cup brown sugar
- 1/2 cup molasses
- 1 egg
- 1/2 teaspoon vanilla extract
- 1 3/4 cups all-purpose flour
- 1 teaspoon baking powder
- 1 teaspoon ground ginger
- 3/4 teaspoon baking soda
- 1/2 teaspoon salt
- 1/2 teaspoon cinnamon
- 1/8 teaspoon ground nutmeg
- 1/8 teaspoon ground cloves
- 2/3 cup boiling water

For the sticky toffee sauce

- 1/2 cup butter
- 1/2 cup granulated sugar
- 1/2 cup brown sugar
- 1/2 cup cream
- A pinch of salt
- 1 teaspoon vanilla extract
- Lightly sweetened whipped cream for serving

continued

1. Preheat oven to 350°F. Spray an 8-inch square cake pan with nonstick baking spray. Set aside.

2. In a large bowl or in the bowl of a stand mixer, beat butter and brown sugar on medium speed until fluffy, 1–2 minutes. Add molasses, egg, and vanilla, and beat just until smooth, scraping down the sides and bottom of the bowl with a rubber spatula as needed. In a medium bowl, combine flour, baking powder, baking soda, ginger, salt, cinnamon, nutmeg, and cloves. With the mixer on low, slowly add the dry ingredients to the mixer and mix just until the dry ingredients are incorporated. With the mixer on low again, add the boiling water to the bowl by slowly pouring the water in a small, steady stream down the inside edge of the bowl. Beat until the batter is smooth, scraping down the sides and bottom of the bowl with a spatula as needed.

3. Pour the batter into the prepared pan and bake for 30–33 minutes until a toothpick poked in the center of the cake comes out clean. Set on a cooling rack to cool.

4. While the cake is cooling, make the sticky toffee sauce. Combine butter, sugars, cream, and salt in a medium saucepan over medium heat. Whisk slowly but constantly until the mixture comes to a simmer then continue cooking for 5 minutes until the sauce is thick and glossy. Remove from heat and stir in vanilla.

5. Serve the cake warm, topped with sticky toffee sauce and lightly sweetened whipped cream.

Resources

I buy lots of pieces—dishes, kitchen linens, utensils, and general doodads—wherever I can find them, whether a chain store or a local boutique. It seems like every town has good vintage and antique shops that you can scour for authentic vintage table linens and kitchen goods, and more and more regular stores are starting to carry new pieces inspired by beautiful vintage finds.

For the photos in the book, props came from the following:

Table Linens

The Little Market
Magnolia
World Market
Target
Local shops

Dishes and Utensils

Williams-Sonoma
World Market
Magnolia
Home Goods
Target
Local shops

Acknowledgments

Huge thanks to my wonderful agent, Lilly Ghahremani at Full Circle Literary, who has been my partner in this project from the very beginning. Thanks to the lovely people at Gibbs Smith who helped make this beautiful book come to life: my editor, Michelle Branson, book designer, Michelle Farinella, and illustrator, Celeste Rockwood-Jones.

Thanks to all of my recipe testers for making sure what I wrote made sense and was easy to follow: Amanda, Amy, Anna Joy, Anna M., Anne, Blair, Caroline, Emily, Heidi, Katie L. Katie R., Kim, Lindsey, Lori, Manda, Merek, Michelle, MJ, Rachel, Sarah, Sommer, Yvonne, and my mom.

To all of my friends who generously let me include their recipes: Tannya, Anne, Annie, Emily and Jared, Amy, Momo and Pop, and most of all, my mom. Similarly, thanks to the friends and family who gave me ideas for recipes and helped me brainstorm. To my extended family and my husband's coworkers for eating so many trial runs, and for always giving honest and unfiltered feedback: thank you!

To the small businesses that let me shoot pictures of their beautiful farms all over Oregon: Petal Pink Flower Farm outside of Eugene; Wooden Shoe Tulip Farm in Woodburn; Thistledown Farm in Junction City; Northern Lights Christmas Tree Farm in Pleasant Hill; and Groundwork Organics in Junction City.

To my BSG ladies for their constant love, support, feedback, and encouragement: I'm so lucky to have a group of inspiring women to learn from and lean on.

And last but not least, thanks to my amazing family. Speedy, Addie, Ellie, James, and George, Mom, Dad, Chaz, Jasmine, Holly, Emily, Thomas, Anna, and all the kids: I love you and am so grateful to be part of such a wonderful family. I'm forever glad we have each other. I love you all. xo

Index

Metric Conversion Chart

Volume Measurements		Weight Measurements		Temperature Conversion	
U.S.	Metric	U.S.	Metric	Fahrenheit	Celsius
1 teaspoon	5 ml	1/2 ounce	15 g	250	120
1 tablespoon	15 ml	1 ounce	30 g	300	150
1/4 cup	60 ml	3 ounces	90 g	325	160
1/3 cup	75 ml	4 ounces	115 g	350	180
1/2 cup	125 ml	8 ounces	225 g	375	190
2/3 cup	150 ml	12 ounces	350 g	400	200
3/4 cup	175 ml	1 pound	450 g	425	220
1 cup	250 ml	2 1/4 pounds	1 kg	450	230

MELISSA BAHEN is the creator of Lulu the Baker, a blog about simple food and modern country life. Her first book, *Scandinavian Gatherings: From Afternoon Fika to Midsummer Feast* came out in 2016 and includes recipes and projects inspired by her beloved Nordic heritage. She and her work have been featured in numerous online and print publications like *Better Homes & Gardens, Sweet Paul, Taproot Magazine,* and *Rachael Ray Every Day.* She lives on a cute, little hobby farm in Western Oregon with her husband, four kids, two bunnies, a flock of chickens, a smart but naughty Aussiedoodle, and a garden much too big to keep up with.